Turn Grief Into Growth - How To Use Dark
Times As A Catalyst For Change

BY ELLA SHAE

© 2023 ALL RIGHTS RESERVED.

Published by She Rises Studios Publishing www.SheRisesStudios.com.

No part of this book may be reproduced or transmitted in any form whatsoever, electronic, or mechanical, including photocopying, recording, or by any informational storage or retrieval system without the expressed written, dated and signed permission from the publisher and co-authors.

LIMITS OF LIABILITY/DISCLAIMER OF WARRANTY:

The co-authors and publisher of this book have used their best efforts in preparing this material. While every attempt has been made to verify the information provided in this book, neither the co-authors nor the publisher assumes any responsibility for any errors, omissions, or inaccuracies.

The co-authors and publisher make no representation or warranties with respect to the accuracy, applicability, or completeness of the contents of this book. They disclaim any warranties (expressed or implied), merchantability, or for any purpose. The co-authors and publisher shall in no event be held liable for any loss or other damages, including but not limited to special, incidental, consequential, or other damages.

ISBN: 978-1-960136-27-5

To anyone who has ever broken me, lied to me, cheated me, stolen from me or watched me self-destruct. To anyone who has hurt me, disappointed me, deceived me or abandoned me. I forgive you and I thank you. You are part of the reason I am who I am today.

For my children. Never settle for anything less than magical. Follow your heart, listen to your soul, and stay true to who you are. In doing so, life can be a beautiful journey.

To my husband. Thank you for loving me in a way I never thought I deserved. In a way I never thought possible. Thank you for loving me despite my chips and cracks.

To my recovery team, no words could describe the gratitude I have for all of you. Not only did you help me navigate through my eating disorder, but you also taught me how to heal from my traumas and become my best self. I am thankful forever.

It is my hope that my story can shed some much needed light on mental illness and create greater mental health awareness.

Spread love, especially to the ones who hurt you, for often they need it the most.

Table of Contents

Introduction 7

1. Yellowbrick Road: To My Younger Self: I'll Be There by Gabriela Bee 10
2. My First Crack: Mean Girls by Leanna Crawford & Praying by Kesha 19
3. Bird Let Out Of The Cage: Gypsy by Fleetwood Mac 27
4. My First 7: Dancing in the Moonlight by Jubël ft. NEIMY 37
5. The Empath And The Narcissist: Something In The Orange by Zach Bryan 45
6. The Rabbit Hole: How Could You by Jessie Murph 58
7. The Empty Casket: Happier Than Ever by Billie Eilish (for my children, Go Easy on Me by Adele) 74
8. It Only Took 13 Years: Wreckage by Nate Smith 83
9. Rainbows, Sunrises and Sunsets: Eyes Closed by Ed Sheeran and The Prayer by Celine Dion 89
10. From Mama to Mommy to Mom to Ma: 5 Leaf Clover by Luke Combs 100
11. COVID…a precursor to my final crack. A chapter on true mental health: TV by Billie Eilish 109
12. Sticks And Stones May Break My Bones: Fly Away by Tones and I 122
13. The Lotus: Love me More by Sam Smith 132
14. Liar Liar Pants On Fire: Self Care by Nicolle Galyon 135

About the Author 142

Before I begin my story, I wanted to provide you with the songs that I associate with specific times in my life. I believe that music and dancing can cure any heartbreak and soothe the soul. I associate so much of my life with music, so it's only fitting that each of my chapters has a song to go with it. I would suggest listening to the song after you read the chapter. The songs are so powerful when you are able to associate them with the story. It took me a while to really pinpoint which songs represented the raw emotions I felt at each time. Music has helped me explore those hard-to-reach places and helped me understand parts of my life that I had buried deep.

Introduction

I want to start by saying that I was welcomed into a family that couldn't wait for my arrival and who loved me and cared for me. They spoiled me and did everything they could to make me happy. The circumstances of my journey are not because I was born into any type of chaos. I didn't start my life with the hardships or obstacles so many others need to overcome. Many begin their journey through struggle. My journey, my OWN journey, really began when I was four years old. At the end of the day, starting off less fortunate really doesn't make a difference. Starting off in an abusive family, homeless, poverty-stricken, addicted… they throw you the curve ball from birth. But make no mistake, I've seen families with the grandest facades have curve balls that they couldn't dodge. Either way, both are ultimately shattering. Starting off good or bad doesn't matter. It's not where you start or where you end. It's the journey to getting there. It's what you choose to do with the ball.

For me, it was an unfortunate event that seemed isolated at the time. It happened, I healed over time, and I could move on. I would have never thought this one particular curve ball would have affected me for 30 years! I'm sure any psychologist might have seen this coming, but I was four and had no idea the impact this really had on me, on my soul, on my entire view of myself, on my self-worth, on my boundaries, and mostly on my own self-love.

The curve balls that life threw at me were hard and fast. I had two choices. I could let them hit me, and I could then blame every other thing that happened to me in my life on that. I could screw up and try less because it wasn't my fault. I could truly believe that I was so unlucky and my actions were a result of what life had handed me. I could, for the rest of my life, use this as an excuse to be an awful person to anyone, simply because if I was to be held accountable for my actions, I could blame it on "what life did to me." I did this for years. It's the path I chose. It was easy to get away with the things I did by blaming anything else. Choice two? Choice two is hard. I didn't even know there was a another choice until I was in my 30s! What I didn't know all those years was that I could use those curve balls to help me grow…To enlighten me… To empower me. It took me 30 years! 30 years to realize I had a choice. It took me 30 years of using those curve balls as excuses for poor behavior. 30 years of thinking I wasn't good enough because of the bumps in the road of my journey. It took me all that time to understand that what the universe threw at me was a lesson. It was something I needed in order to be a better person. It happened to give me perspective.

Each chapter is dedicated to a significant point in my life that affected my mental health and what I've learned from it as an adult. No matter how rocky the roads were along my journey, I wouldn't change a thing. One slight difference can change your whole trajectory, and I love my path. I love who I am today, despite the hardships it took to get here. I would relive every moment if I had to; I would just do it with a different mindset or perspective.

My hope is that anyone who reads this learns, grows, and becomes enlightened. Hopefully, for you, it's sooner than 30 years. My story probably hits home for many people of any age. It certainly wasn't easy for me to revisit these moments. If I can help even one person with my advice and experience, then rehashing it all is worth it. My hope is that one day you will become the voice for the next person, and eventually the stigma of mental health will be silenced with our voices! **Mental Health IS Health**!

My journey, which you are about to experience and may relate to in some way, is based on first-hand experiences with:
- Bullying
- Suicidal thoughts
- Substance abuse to silence anxiety
- How family dynamics influence your decisions
- Narcissism
- Divorce and starting over
- Mental, emotional, and physical abuse
- Abortions, births, and losses
- Grief in losing loved ones
- The psychological effect of Covid on my family
- Anorexia
- Eating disorder recovery
- Low self esteem and self worth
- Parenting

I wish all who read this peace, love, light, and happiness. XO
Ella Shae
www.ellashae.com
info@ellashae.com

Yellowbrick Road

The year was 1986, and my parents, my six month old sister and I had just moved into our new house. My father had built our house from the ground up. There were not many houses around us at the time. We were one of the first to build. Years later, the development would become quite a coveted area. It had a huge backyard with a deck and hot tub. It had an in-ground pool and the best part—my own room. I was four years old and none of this mattered to me. What mattered was that my best friend lived only a few houses away. She was my best friend all throughout high school, and it all started when we were in pre-school. We went to the same private school together, a catholic school about 10 minutes from our houses. It's important to know that every single road to this school was a side street. There was only one "main" road that was pretty busy on the way to that school. Most days, my mom and Layla's mom would take turns taking us to school. We even had a friend who lived a few blocks down on Yellow Brick Road, to be exact. Her mom was a part of the carpool as well. Between the three of them, my mom rarely had to take my little sister out in the cold winter months. Which, as a mother myself now, is a huge score. Bundling a newborn up for a ten minute drive in the winter is at the bottom of my list of things I want to do. On this particular day, Layla's mother was on pick-up duty. She would swing past my house and then down a couple of blocks to pick up our other little friend. Then we would head off to school. Katie (my friend's mother) drove a brand new Volvo. It was literally the safest car you could buy at the time. I'm not even being dramatic. It ACTUALLY was.

On the way to school, we would always play *I Spy* games. Those ten minutes to school flew by! Around 8am, Katie pulled into my driveway, and I ran to the car. Layla was behind her mom in the back seat, so I ran to the other side. Before I could even buckle my seatbelt, Layla shouted, "I spy something blue!" We were already playing our game as Katie drove off to pick up the third kiddo on Yellowbrick Road. I couldn't find anything blue for the life of me. I scooted into the middle of the back seat to look out of the windshield. This is all I can remember from that day. My next memory of that day isn't actually a memory. It's a smell. The smell of iodine. Whenever I retell this story or think about it, this smell comes to my mind. Whenever someone uses iodine on me or around me, I get an awful feeling associated with this day in 1986 on Yellowbrick Road.

I know that in your later years of life, it's very hard to remember things that happened at four years old. In fact, up until three years old, it's been scientifically proven that most adults don't have any real memories from those first three years. You may think you remember things, but most times that memory is actually a story you've heard your mom tell before or a photograph you saw from that day. You mistake those for the actual memory when, in reality, you don't usually remember much from that young of an age. I can tell you this. I remember some things from the days that followed. I have a blurry memory of a man with a long beard picking me up out of the car. I remember my uncle giving me a stuffed horse that seemed enormous at the time. I remember being pushed in a wheelchair down a hall. I remember the smell of iodine. I remember the sound of a woman's voice. I remember a box of handmade cards being dropped off at my house that all my classmates had made for me. My teacher dropped them off and even stayed to visit me. I remember the feel of the stitches on my face. But what I remember most is the day my grandmother convinced me to look at myself in the mirror.

The rest of the story has been pieced together for me by my parents and family.

I spy something blue. To this day, when my kids want to play *I Spy*, I get a subconscious feeling of dread as if something bad is about to happen. I never knew why I had that nagging feeling until I forced myself to recall as many of that day's events as I could. As I was looking for something blue, Katie drove down Yellowbrick Road. A man driving a postal truck had run a stop sign and essentially almost killed me. This wasn't your regular mailman. This postal truck delivered the bins of mail to individual post offices. He was running late, so he decided to cut through some side streets to make up time. Not only did he run the stop sign, but he ran the stop sign at 30 miles per hour. The point of impact? Exactly where I was sitting. The Volvo collapsed like an accordion and took me down with it.

My father retells the story to me with some pieces left out, just as my mother does. I think it's the brain's way of coping. Your brain blocks out pieces of traumas so that you can recover from them. It's a defense mechanism to protect itself. It is called dissociation—or detachment from reality. It's fascinating, actually. The brain will wander off during the event, so some parts can not be recollected. Unfortunately, the brain doesn't forget everything in a trauma, at least not in most cases. Each of my parents retells the story with all the major details exactly the same. However, each of them remembers parts of the story that the other does not. It's likely because each of them had dissociation at different times. For me, it's different. I have almost complete amnesia when it comes to that day. Yes, I was very young, so chances are I wouldn't have remembered much anyway, but despite my age, there is a theory that my brain has repressed those negative memories. That theory suggests when the brain creates memories in a state of trauma, most of the time they are inaccessible unless in that exact state of trauma again. This explains my fear of driving, especially being in a car with other drivers, still at 38 years old.

My parents received the phone call regarding my accident and were at the scene within minutes. My father describes what he saw. Police officers and EMTs crowded around the car. Another police officer held them back while stating I was alive but unsure of the extent of my injuries until they could pull me out. As the jaws of life pried me out from underneath the crushed car, the police officer allowed my parents to run toward me. He then said how the EMT worked on me and then sent me straight to the hospital. My mother recalls the day with a slight difference. She received the call, and they arrived within minutes. The EMT held me and tried to stop my face from bleeding. They took off my winter hat, stained with blood and filled with glass. She climbed into the back of the ambulance and held me the entire way to the hospital while I cried in pain. Both stories are correct, except for the dissociation of each experience. My mother blocked out the jaws of life while my father blocked out the details of what happened AFTER the jaws of life. It was almost like my father needed to see I was okay and pulled out of that car before his brain could wander. My mothers' brain wouldn't register what was happening UNTIL she saw me in her arms.

So what was my condition when I was pulled out from underneath the heap of metal that was once the safest car of 1986? The entire right side of my face was mangled. In the 80s the frame around a car window was metal. Today it's that black, rubbery, foam piece, but not then. Not even on the safest car of 1986. That metal frame sliced open the right side of my face instantly. I don't just mean lacerations. I mean full-blown sliced my cheek open, if not off. I had an open wound through all layers of my skin, from my eye to my nose and down to my lip. The window shattered, and all of the glass pieces flew into my already torn open face. The impact and being trapped broke my collarbone.

from broken to beautifully broken

The man with the beard was the officer who arrived at the scene. My family never told me the details of that day. What happened to the postal driver? Was Katie screaming in terror? Was the neighborhood all outside watching? Who called 911? I always thought my parents believed those were details I didn't need to know. In reality, it was simply too hard for them to recall or relive the details of that day. The ambulance pulled into the emergency room at 9am. My parents were told by the surgeon on call that morning that I needed a plastic surgeon—a good, highly recommended plastic surgeon—if they wanted the best chance of my face resembling normalcy. This wasn't just stitches; it was reconstruction. The job was only for someone with experience performing plastic surgery with fine detail and skill. They tried their best to get me a surgeon who would put my face back together like it was only an hour ago. The plastic surgeon they chose was on the other side of the United States in California. He would not be available until 9 pm. We spent 12 hours in the emergency room waiting, picking pieces of glass out of my wounds and putting ice on my face so that it wouldn't start to heal and impede the surgical process. Three hours later, I came out of surgery with over 500 stitches throughout the many layers of my face and my eye sewn shut. My surgeon reattached pieces of my nose and lip. My eyelid had a laceration from the glass, so it had to be sewn closed in order for the stitched wound to heal. I know the emotional and psychological effects this day had on me now, but in that moment I had no idea. At that moment, I didn't realize that this day also had a lasting impact on my family. As a mother, I can't even imagine holding my four year old in a blood-drenched coat with her face the way mine was.

I spent five days in the hospital. My memory of the stuffed animal, the horse, was from my uncle. He brought it on one of the many times he visited. My whole family visited. They were so upset, and I had no clue why. I didn't understand at that age the depth or magnitude that an event like this has on you. They all knew. They knew that I had a long road ahead. However, I don't think they were even thinking about what my life would be 10-15 years from then. They had not even thought that far ahead. They were simply worried about the next few months. Imagine the fear they would have felt if they really knew what the next 20-30 years were like for me!

The woman's voice. No one can really tell me for sure who that voice belonged to, but I imagine it was my nurse. She would talk to me in this very quiet, calm voice. She would ask me to try and open my healthy eye to no avail. Yes, a majority of the time I spent in the hospital, I had both eyes closed. One of them was perfectly fine, yet I kept it closed. You see, when you have an injury to one eye, you can sometimes have what is called a sympathizing eye. The healthy eye is called the "sympathizing eye" because it actually becomes inflamed. She tried every day, and every day I refused to force that eye open. I wonder if that's why the memories I have are foggy. Was it because my vision was ACTUALLY foggy? Perhaps it's because they are tiny snippets of that week that are fading in my memory. I wish the impact of this day had faded away quickly, but I wasn't so lucky.

The day I left the hospital, I remember being pushed in a wheelchair. My nurse leaned down one last time and said, "Let me see those beautiful eyes before you leave me." And I let her. I opened my one eye for the briefest second, but it was a milestone. I was making progress, and I made her day. On the way home, I kept my eyes closed. I kept my eyes closed when my father carried me into the house. I kept my eyes closed when they laid me on the couch. I kept my eyes closed when my grandmother cried. My grandmother had been living with us at the time to help my mother care for me and my sister. She hadn't seen me yet since she was home with my sister while my parents stayed with me at the hospital. She wasn't prepared for what she saw. In the upcoming days, my grandmother would try to lighten the mood. She worked on getting me to open my eyes every day, with no luck.

The box of cards. This memory is pretty vivid. I wonder if it's because it was after the trauma. My preschool teacher came to my house to drop off a box of cards all my classmates had handmade for me. I recognized her voice immediately. I LOVED this teacher. She might be in my top three of all the teachers I've had. The moment I heard her voice, I opened my eyes. I opened my eyes to see her and to see all those cards! I must have been craving the normalcy of my life pre-accident. I wanted to be in school. I wanted to see all my friends and classmates and her coming over gave me a little piece of that. I'll never forget sitting at the top of the steps that led to my basement, looking at the drawings and writing on every single card (I was four so teacher-guided writing, of course). I took them out one-by-one and smiled. My life was getting back to normal.

Once I had opened my eyes, my family knew I would eventually see myself in a mirror. Up until then, I had felt the stitches on my face. It was like hundreds of little threads sticking out of me. Porcupine is the word that explains my feelings now as I recall it. At some point, I would walk past a mirror, and my grandmother didn't want me to see my face the first time alone. She walked with me to the bathroom, and we looked in the mirror. I swear I was wearing pink leggings, but no one remembers that. I remember, though. I remember because what I saw horrified me, and the only thing my brain could do to protect me was to stare at my pants in the mirror instead of my face. As you may have guessed, I needed to see a therapist. I was having nightmares, and I would not even entertain getting into a car. What's amazing is that after only a few visits, the nightmares stopped, and I found it easier to get into the car after each session. After enough time had passed, I went to the surgeon to remove the stitches. My mother tells me that I was not a happy camper. I screamed and kicked the whole time. It was getting to the point where the doctor told my mother that they would need to hold me down in some strange contraption if I didn't sit still. It wasn't because they were frustrated with me, but because 500 stitches took hours. Add resistance to that, and we would be there for days!

One look at that thing, and I stayed as quiet as I could. I still made it difficult for the doctor, but at least I wasn't flailing my arms and legs any longer. They decided it was better to go a few times to remove the stitches to give me a break. Once those stitches were out, the trauma was over. I literally went right back to being a kid. It was like the whole thing never happened. Like I mentioned earlier: It happened, I healed, I moved on. That is until middle school.

What I Know Now

Up until middle school, I didn't really think much about beauty. I don't remember even once wondering if I was pretty or if I was tall or skinny. Was dark hair attractive? Were my hazel, yellow eyes different? I had no idea because I did not actually care! I did not think about the clothes I wore or the shoes I had. My mother picked out all my outfits, shoes and even haircuts. I'll omit the part in my story where my mother gave me a haircut that looked like a bowl on my head. Like a mushroom cut for little boys… except I was a girl. Yea, not even that bothered me at the time. She often matched my outfits with my younger sister, and I never said a word about it. For me, it was more about having the coolest bike or the cutest baby dolls. I also needed the stroller so I could walk my baby dolls to my best friend's house every day after school. For a greater portion of my life, I wondered lots of "what ifs'." What if I had taken a little bit longer to walk down the steps of my house to Katie's car? What if we weren't playing the *I Spy* game and I hadn't scooted to the middle seat? What if I had my seatbelt on? What if the postmaster had just been on time?! What if I had just stayed home that freezing cold March day? What if Layla and I had never become friends? What if it was my mom's turn to drive? God, I wasted so many nights staring at the ceiling in bed and thinking of all the scenarios where I would have led a completely different life. I felt sorry for myself and thought: why me? Of all the people in the world,

from broken to beautifully broken

I had to be in the direct contact point of this mail truck. Why would God do this to me?

Today I would tell my 13-year-old self that I was asking the wrong questions all along. I was wondering about the what if and the why me, but really I should have focused on what the universe was trying to teach me. All these years, I wondered why God did this to me, but that got me nowhere. There was no answer to those questions. No matter how many times I asked them, no one could ever answer them. I had to change my perspective. Maybe that car accident was caused by complete and total bad luck. Maybe God didn't do this to me, but instead, maybe he saved me. Maybe I was going to die in that accident. Maybe I would have been paralyzed. Maybe if I wasn't in the world's safest car, I would have lost an arm or a leg when I was crushed. Maybe God couldn't stop the accident, but maybe all the things that led up to it saved me. Maybe I needed to start thinking about how lucky I was. What I needed to do was change my mindset. I needed to be grateful for all the ways I was saved! I could be dead, or my injuries could have been far worse. I could have had a plastic surgeon that wasn't as good as mine, leaving my face unrecognizable. You see, it's not the curveball that life throws at you. It's what you do with the ball.

I challenge you to change your perspective. When you are falling down that dark rabbit hole and the negative thoughts have you cycling out of control, CHANGE YOUR PERSPECTIVE. Focus on the positive. Find something you can pull out of your situation that you are thankful for. For me, I learned to be grateful that I was alive to experience this amazing life I have created for myself. I am grateful that even after all the stitches, I am still beautiful. Change your mindset. Change your perspective. Find the good and be grateful. The universe has so much more to give to you if you try.

My First Crack

In all the years that passed after the accident, I never thought about my scar. Yes, I thought my mom was so annoying when she loaded my face up with zinc before we went on the beach or before I played outside, but I never thought about my scar. My scar was a part of me. I grew up with my scar. I didn't know my face without it! It wasn't weird to me that I had it on my cheek and none of my other siblings or friends did. I honestly did not even notice it until one day at recess. I was still in that same catholic school and had just approached the final months of seventh grade. At this point, the desire to send your kids to catholic school had faded, and I had nine kids in my class, five girls and four boys. Three of the four boys were dating three of the five girls. Guess who no one was dating, me. I didn't care one bit about that because those four boys were not attractive to me in any sense, and dating was not something I was interested in. I was still playing manhunt with the kids on the block and riding our bikes after school. Who the heck would want a boyfriend? Not me, that's for sure! The three "couples" and the rest of us were all playing basketball together, and I missed one of the shots (I am the least athletic person in existence). I giggled, knowing it was typical of me, but one of the boys said something that started my first "crack." It was my life's second curve ball.

"Jesus, scarface, can't you make the shot?" Scarface. It was the first

from broken to beautifully broken

time I had ever heard that word referencing me.

Many would say that my first crack would have been the accident itself. That wasn't a crack. That was a curveball, but that accident proved me to be a survivor. The accident itself didn't break me. What came from it years later did. All I know is that I didn't feel this kind of pain in the accident. What I felt then was physical pain. What I felt now was emotionally unbearable.

I had never experienced this type of emotion. I am not even sure there is a word for this emotion. His voice was playing over and over in my head. I felt lightheaded, and I could hear my pulse in my ears. I had a lump in my throat and a confused look on my face. The playground was spinning. The girls immediately ran toward me, seeing that I was processing what had just happened and feared how I would react. So many things immediately ran through my head. Did everyone notice my scar? Is that why none of the boys wanted to date me? Am I ugly? Was everyone secretly calling me this awful nickname, and if so, did people identify me as scarface? Was it really that weird that I had this scar? Do they even know why I had this scar? My head was spinning with thoughts, and the only thing I could do was run. I don't remember exactly where I went until the recess teacher rang her big gold bell, but I know my stomach hurt thinking I would have to walk back into a room with these kids until the day was over. I decided I needed to get out of there. I went to the nurse and told her my stomach hurt. Not a REAL lie, considering my stomach felt like I got punched in it. My mom came to pick me up early, and she immediately saw I was visibly upset. She probably gave me some sort of pep talk after I told her what the boy said. She probably tried to console me and tell me that I was beautiful. I don't remember. I do remember my mom coming to the school the next day and jumping out of the car when she saw this boy. She told him if he ever called me that again, she would chase him with her frying pan. Sounds completely abnormal, but the boy was scared. Probably more so because our moms were friends.

Unfortunately, he wasn't scared enough. He continued to call me that new nickname, except now it was behind my back. I would hear the whispers or the laughs and know it was something they were saying about me. I never said a word about it again. Not to my mother, teacher, or even the girls who were my friends. The more I ignored it, the more I could pretend it wasn't happening.

In a school this small it was hard to do any of the fun stuff that most public schools could do. We didn't have an eighth grade trip to Washington or the teen canteens that other middle schools had. Instead, we had "dances." The sixth, seventh and eighth grade students in my catholic school would join other catholic schools and have dances in the auditoriums. Once a month, different schools hosted, and most times, we would have refreshments and some speakers on the stage playing music. Once in a while, a slow song would play, and people would dance together. This was the kind of slow dance that makes me cringe today. The girl's hands are on the boy's shoulders while his hands are wrapped around her waist, and they sway back and forth, barely moving their feet. SO WEIRD! Today, I may think of this type of dancing in a bad light because no one had ever asked me to dance. Not just from my own catholic school, but from the others as well. There could have been a hundred different reasons why no one asked me to dance, but at 12 years old, the only one I could think of was my scar. The scar that once was so insignificant to me was now the answer to everything I questioned. Just. Like. That. It only took one boy to ruin me for years to come. Just to be clear, today, I hate that I even give him this much credit for what happened in my life. However, if I am being honest and telling my complete truth, this was the start of my snowball of issues for years to come.

I graduated eighth grade at my catholic school and decided I wanted to continue with private school for my high school years. Of the nine students, four of us went to the same private high school. On the first day of school, my stomach was in knots. I actually felt my hands shaking when I got dropped off at the front of the building. For a few minutes before school actually began, everyone would stand and chat on the front steps and front lawn. I was so nervous. Where would I stand? Who would I talk to until the doors opened? Was my uniform being worn in the same way as the other girls who looked popular? I legit was petrified that I wasn't going to make any friends. I was so nervous that people wouldn't like me or that they would think I was a loser. I didn't walk into that catholic school on the first day with the people who I was in elementary and middle school with. I went alone. The only hope I had was to see one of them and stand with them. As I walked up the five or so stairs towards the building, which felt like I was climbing the stairs of a lighthouse, I smiled at every single person I saw. A smile was inviting right? A smile lets people know that you are one of the nice ones. A smile invited conversation. A smile showed "It's my first day, and I know no one, so PLEASE invite me to stand with you and your friends." Nope. Nothing. I did spot one of the girls I had gone to school with, and as I approached her, she turned her back. Her older brother had gone to this school, so she already knew a ton of people. I moved over to the far corner of the steps. No one was around me, and if I stood quiet enough, no one would notice me. As the minutes passed, I became more and more nervous. I gave up on trying to introduce myself to people. Everyone was already formed into little cliques, and I had no place in any of them. The only thing more embarrassing than smiling at someone and watching them turn around as if they didn't even see you, is standing ALONE. If I stood in that little corner, then maybe I would be invisible enough that no one even noticed me. Once the doors opened, things didn't get any better. We had to go directly to the gym and sit on the bleachers for an opening day speech from the Father of the school. Great! Another time I'd have to find a corner to be unnoticeable. I sat down, and a girl my age turned towards me and looked right at me! Finally, someone who wants to get to know who I am! I introduced myself, and instead of her then telling me her name, she asked me if I minded scooting over because she was saving the seat. Awesome. Day one down and 179 more to go.

Some days were okay, some days were worse. Throughout my freshman year, MOST of my days I went unnoticed, which I was more than happy to be so long as I wasn't being the target of someone's jokes. Don't get me wrong, I was teased and taunted every week of the entire school year. As this happened more and more often, my self-confidence began to plummet. I felt like I had nothing to look forward to. The kids in my grade would go to parties and hang out on the weekends, and I had Blockbuster with my dad and some new CDs to play on my boombox. This should have been enough. I should have been enough. But it wasn't. I started to feel worse and worse about myself. I stopped eating lunch at school mostly because I sat alone and refused to walk into the cafeteria and sit alone anymore but also because, in my mind, if my face was ugly, I could at least make sure my body looked good. This, as you could imagine, turned into an eating disorder many years later. In fact, as I write this I still struggle with food, with eating in front of people, and with staying skinny so the focus isn't on my face. At a certain point, starving myself to be able to control an aspect of my life was no longer working. I started to think it would be easier NOT to wake up and go to school just to be tormented on one day or invisible on another. What was the point of all this? I couldn't find joy in anything in my life. I sat in my room one night and willed myself to think of five things I looked forward to. Five reasons staying alive mattered. I couldn't do it. In that moment, nothing mattered except escaping this groundhog's day of life in high school. I like to think I wouldn't have gone through with actually killing myself regardless of what happened next, but my brother and sister stopped me dead in my tracks. My sister was only about ten, and my brother eight. They came into my room and asked me if I was coming to play family game night. My dad had set up the kitchen table with Parcheesi, and they wanted me to join. That was my enlightenment. That was my pivotal moment.

These were my reasons. I had a family that loved me and that even on my worst day, they would always show up. They would make me smile. They would give me something to look forward to. Parcheesi! Can you imagine in a million years that my life changed on a Friday night all because my dad sent my brother and sister to come and get me to play Parcheesi! For them, they thought they were just having our normal family fun night, but for me, they saved me from making an awful mistake. A mistake I could have never taken back. The next morning I sat with my parents and told them I was ready to try out public school when the new year started. I needed a clean slate in a place where no one knew me. After all, what could be worse than what I had already gone through?

What I Know Now

Middle school and my freshman year in high school had very few moments of happiness. I can't sit here and say there were none, but the hurt and the effects of this trauma outweighed those happy moments. I did have two really great friends in high school that always made me laugh. If you guys are reading this, I want to thank you for sometimes being my only reason to smile. I wouldn't have made it through that year without you both. So…What would I tell myself now if I could go back in time?

Again, it's not the curveballs life throws at you, it's what you do with the ball. Always choose joy. Choose to embrace your style. You can wallow, or you can choose what makes you happy. For so many years of my life, I allowed those boys to dictate my level of happiness. I missed out on so many things. Instead, I could've used those experiences to make myself a better person. I didn't need revenge. I didn't need to prove myself. I just needed confidence. I needed self-love. I am saddened as I think of all the activities I missed out on all those years. I allowed them that control in my life.

As you can imagine, most of my life was filled with anxiety. I was always worried about what would happen when I walked into a classroom, or who was going to ask me to dance. But instead of worrying about the what ifs in the future, I should have just enjoyed and appreciated the things I had in the present moment. You see, you can't control everything in your life. In fact, most things you can't control at all. But you can control your reaction. Instead of feeling sorry for myself all these years, I should have wondered why these boys needed to pick on me. I should have focused on what was good in my life. Not what was crushing my spirit. You can't control the actions of others. You can't control how they treat you. But you can control how you react to it. You can control what you will allow in your life and what you will not. You certainly can control your own happiness, and you should NEVER allow someone else to have that control, especially when there is so little in life we can control in the first place! All those years, I made the wrong choice.

What would I tell my younger self? I would tell myself to sit back and think of the positive things I have in my life. Thinking of all the positive and good things will always outweigh the hardships. I suggest in moments of self-doubt to think of five positive things. It could be your traits. It could be your skills or talents. It could be things you have. Anything, really. The harder you train your mind to focus on the good things in life instead of the bad, the faster it will become an automatic instinct. The brain will bypass the negative and immediately focus on the good in that moment. Before you begin rewriting your thoughts, I need to warn you that this doesn't happen overnight. It takes time, effort and patience. You will have negative thoughts. You will respond to negative situations for quite some time. The work is acknowledging it, stopping it and redirecting. There will always be people who test your strength in this area. People will push your buttons, and you will need to use every fiber of your being to respond in a way that's best for your own self-worth, self esteem and confidence.

The process is not linear, but it does become easier.

Today, when I feel defeated or come across someone who doesn't treat me the way I expect, I don't get mad. I try to understand their perspective and why they're acting this way toward me before I respond. Words are just words if you have self-love. If you know your worth, then what they say is just words coming out of their mouth. They don't hold any weight. A very wise person, my best friend and soul sister, once told me: "Hurt people, hurt people." Remember that phrase the next time someone hurts you. Have empathy. Change your perspective. Look outside of yourself and see their side. You can't control them, but you CAN control your reaction. What will you do with the ball?

Bird Let Out Of The Cage

The summer before sophomore year, I spent most days prepping for my life's new big change. I got contacts instead of glasses. I went shopping for real clothes instead of uniforms, and most importantly, I had a procedure done called dermabrasion. My original plastic surgeon had told my parents that at some point down the line, we could smooth out some of the lines and raised scars on my face, but that it wasn't necessary until I asked for it. This was the summer I asked for it. The procedure was quick. Same day, in and out. Maybe two to three weeks of recovery with no sun on the new skin. This was my shot at a clean slate. No one knew me in this school besides my best friend down the street. I was nervous, anxious and mostly excited.

On the first day of my new public school, I had the same anxiety from last year's first day of school. Every single fear I had from last year came to the surface once again. The only difference with this time was that I did have someone to walk in with, my best friend. Instead of smiling at everyone and trying to make everyone want to be my friend, I walked into that building with a stone-cold face. I actually don't think that I even knew I wasn't smiling. It was like my body went into crisis management, and I was on autopilot. My body language screamed confidence mixed with a little mystery. On that very first day of school, in the very first steps I took into the building, I was surrounded by people. Mostly boys. The girls stood close by with looks on their faces like they had to solve the mystery in the next Nancy Drew book.

"Who is she? Where did she come from? How old is she? Did she just move to town? Does she have a boyfriend?" The questions were thrown at my best friend left and right as if I couldn't speak for myself. With a voice I had to pull from the depths of my stomach, I answered them all.

"Ella. I came from a catholic school. I am 15. I've always lived here. And no." Within seconds boy after boy introduced themselves. Okay, to be fair, it was more like five or six boys, but to me, it felt like 100. A few of the girls were so kind to me, and they are still my friends today. The other girls didn't like that I was the "fresh meat" and stealing all the attention. As each class passed, I had more and more people introduce themselves. Word spread about me before I even made it to lunch. I was invited to my first party that weekend, and I had a seat at a table with PEOPLE at lunch. I was officially cool. People liked me. Now I had to figure out what in the world one does when attending a high school party.

I was on cloud nine. Seriously. I had people who wanted to be my friends, guys who asked for my phone number AND I was going to my first "kegger." I went to my best friend's house after school, and she gave me a crash course on how to be cool. I couldn't blow this!

During that week, I allowed the boys to exchange numbers with me, but no way in hell was I calling them. I was way too nervous for that, and I wasn't ready to deal with that kind of anxiety. To my surprise, this made the boys call me and chase after me more! More and more girls I had classes with warmed up to me, and I had some really great friendships already beginning. Friday came way faster than I was ready for. I changed my outfit 1,000 times and finally walked to Layla's house so we could go together. We were 15, so we still needed someone to drive us around. Uber did not exist then, unfortunately. Both of our moms drove us to the party, and we were ADAMANT about them dropping us off a block away so no one saw us get out of our parent's car. We actually asked them to wear hats as well, but that deal was off the table.

I was physically ill. My hands were shaking, my stomach was in knots and I think my teeth were chattering, not from being cold but from having an actual panic attack. So much weighed on what happened that night. What if people saw through my facade and realized I was a loser? This was make it or break it, and if I didn't make it, I had no other schools to run to. I would have to stick this one out for three more years, whether I liked it or not. I guess I could also make my parents move, right?

I walked into the party and was greeted with a red Solo cup filled with the most disgusting smelling beer. Think skunk in a cup. As it was handed to me, the beer sloshed around in the cup and spilled all over the place. Music was blasting, and people were everywhere. The front yard was filled with people, the backyard and even the inside of the house! People were smoking weed in the backyard and doing keg stands in the far corner. I would secretly spill a little of my beer every step I took, so it looked like I drank that cup of cheap beer. When people asked me if I wanted to smoke, I just replied with, "Yeah, in a little bit." You see, I WAS still the same girl as last year, but to make it through high school, I had to fit in with these people.

As the months passed, I would still have anxiety when I missed a party or couldn't meet on the side street after school to smoke weed. I was nervous if the girls got together with the boys at someone's house and I couldn't make it. If I missed something that happened, I would be an outsider when they talked about it the next day. Too many times of not being able to make it, and I probably wouldn't even get invited anymore. I was so scared that with one small mistake, with one wrong move, I would go back to being scarface. I was spiraling with anxiety. In actuality, I had more anxiety now than the previous year. Last year I was at rock bottom. This year I had something to lose. I could not go backward and needed to start engaging in some activities I previously avoided. It was the only way to stay relevant. Halfway through sophomore year is when it all changed for me. I became a popular girl, and I now played the part well. My pants got tighter, skirts shorter and tops smaller. I dyed my hair and went tanning. I secretly got my belly button pierced and went to NYC to get a tattoo. I dated boys that were popular even though I didn't like them. I got my nails done, and not only did I not miss a party, I started throwing my own. I would sneak people into my basement windows so they could hide all the alcohol they brought from my parents. I mastered keg stands and making Os while I blew out the smoke from my cigarettes. I was a pro at rolling joints or packing bowls, and I knew all the people to buy from. I would leave school during lunch periods with the seniors to have liquid lunches. That was when you drank alcohol for lunch and then chewed an entire pack of gum before heading back into the building. Which, by the way, was not easy. It was like real-life 007 finding the door we left open with a book to get back in and avoid the cameras. I had a pager to match every pair of pants and always carried a pack of cigarettes in the waistband of my pants. I was no longer pretending to be cool. I was cool. I was like a bird let out of its cage. I had newfound popularity, and I didn't know how to reign it in. The thing is, I didn't ACTUALLY like smoking or drinking. I did it to keep my anxiety at ease. I was constantly worried about making sure I was still cool. My anxiety level was a ten, constantly thinking about the choices I had to make to stay relevant. When I drank or smoked, my anxiety lessened. I didn't worry as much, and life was just easier.

 I'm sure my parents didn't love what they saw, but to be completely honest, I don't think they even knew half of what I did. Sure, they found out about the obvious. The parties at the house, the change in clothing, but I always tried to convince them that this was how all teenagers were. They didn't buy it and would ground me. I then figured out ways to convince them to UNground me. It usually worked, mostly because they were so annoyed with me and finally gave in. Anxiety can make you very persistent.

Around my junior year, "clubbing" became a thing among my friends. I was only 16, and most of the clubs were 18 to get in. Luckily I knew a kid who made fake IDs and most of my friends were promoters at these clubs. Let me remind you, my level of anxiety never disappeared. I was always thinking one step ahead. I was worried about getting in trouble or suddenly becoming irrelevant when another new girl started school, and now with these fake IDs and clubbing, I was really nervous we might even get arrested. But I swallowed my anxiety and kept a straight face. Towards the end of my junior year and the beginning of my senior year, ecstasy was everywhere. I mean *everywhere.* Kids would take it and go to school. Most people would wait until the weekend and get a ton of these pills and head into the city. I would tell my parents I was sleeping at a friend's house, and my friend would tell her parents she was sleeping at my house. Freedom. Freedom for the entire night with no one to answer to.

Most of the "cool" kids in our town would head into the city on the weekends and stay in these clubs until 6:00 or 7:00 am! Some were truly dedicated to these places and stayed till the next afternoon even. A majority of the nights, we were on the guest list of most clubs we went to, so we walked right in. We had a full body search, and that was it. The night was ours. Every corner of these clubs had house dealers selling ecstasy. I never wanted to try it because, again, anxiety. This particular time my friend, who I trusted, told me it was safe. He told me that he had done it before and was totally fine. Plus, there was an entire VIP section of our friends there with me. All of which had already swallowed these pills. I looked at the girls I went with and decided, why not. Everyone I knew had done it, and every single one said how amazing it was. In one small sip of water, I had officially added another thing to my list of ways to stay relevant.

It took a little bit, but when that pill worked, for the first time in years, I had no anxiety. I had pure happiness. No worries. No regrets. No thinking about what was coming next. No thinking at all! Just pure bliss. I felt the weight of the past three years lift off my soul and mind, and I finally felt at peace. Okay, look, I know that it wasn't a permanent thing. I knew at some point this feeling would end and rip me back into my vicious cycle of spiraling thoughts. But for just a few hours, I got a break. My friends and I visited these clubs often. We did ecstasy often. The problem with this drug was that it would last for hours. Sometimes I didn't have hours. Sometimes I had to actually head home, and if I walked in with pupils the size of pennies, my parents would lose their shit. Have you ever gone to a New York City club sober? MOST. AWFUL. EXPERIENCE. When you're not on drugs and everyone else is, they look so incredibly stupid. I would rather stay home if I didn't have an entire night of freedom. If that was the case, then I needed something else. I needed something to erase my thoughts and give my mind a break.

I dabbled with a few things here and there to try and find relief from my anxiety. Sometimes it worked. Sometimes it made it worse. At the end of the day, no matter which drugs or how many drugs I did, I always eventually returned back to my feelings of anxiety. It was a vicious disorder, and no one knew I had it. I told a few people about it, and their response was to just think about something else and to stop driving myself crazy. They would tell me that I caused my own anxiety and that I needed to just stop worrying. Clearly, at that time, no one around me knew about mental health and mental disorders, but neither did I. PTSD wasn't even a diagnosis until 1980, and even then, it was used mostly as a diagnosis for soldiers in war. I wonder how my life may have been different had there been more known outlets for people with mental illnesses. The problem I was now facing was what started as something to do to stay in the in-crowd had now become my crutch when the anxiety was just too much.

What I Know Now

Well, first, I wanted to turn back time and go back and shake myself. How could I be so stupid? I could have DIED at the expense of being cool. As a matter of fact, I had three friends die of overdoses during my years at high school and at least a dozen more throughout my life. As I reflected on the three short years I spent in public school, I couldn't help but feel disappointed and somewhat disgusted. I say disgusted because as I relive those moments in my head, I actually get a feeling of nausea that sweeps over me. I tried changing my perspective of myself all those years and looked through the lens of empathy.

I needed to understand why I engaged in these activities before I could forgive myself for abusing my body. It boils down to two words: Mental Health. It could be very easy for me to sit here and say that I engaged in all those activities because I was emotionally abused. I was taunted, I was bullied, I was an outcast. I could use all those things as an excuse for why I made awful decisions in my teenage years. But the truth is, I wasn't just acting out or trying to get attention. I was suffering from a mental illness that was going unnoticed by so many for so long! If I was suffering for all those years and not even my family noticed, not even my best friends, then how many others in this world are suffering this silent battle? I self-medicated for years, trying to rid myself of anxiety and depression, even if it were for only a few short hours. The irony is that one of my biggest anxiety triggers is death, and everything I was doing to avoid being anxious over the concept of death could have actually killed me. I was a teenager and didn't know how to handle my mental health. This is not something to blame my parents for, my teachers or friends, or even the people who made me suffer all those years! The only thing to be blamed, besides my ignorance, is the lack of information and awareness on mental health. No one could help me if no one REALLY knew about the disease. PTSD was barely known to anyone outside of the mental health field. No one knew about depression and anxiety because they were taboo when I was a teenager. It meant you would need to see a psychiatrist, and god forbid that! That meant you were crazy. Any person in high school that saw a psychiatrist was labeled crazy. And let me be very clear, the only ones who actually went to the psychiatrist that we knew of were the ones who did outrageous things. To high schoolers, psychiatrists equaled crazy. Even to adults! If a parent told another parent that their child needed to take medication or needed therapy, those parents JUDGED. They judged the child, and they judged the parents. Because if you were a good parent, your kid wouldn't need therapy. WRONG! No matter how well you were brought up or how much trauma you experienced, mental illness is a disease. It is a sickness that so much of America didn't buy into because you couldn't "see" it. I unfortunately did not have the proper channels available to me to address my brain's health, but if, as a society, we end this stigma associated with having mental health disorders, then we may actually be giving today's generation a chance at something we never had.

What I Know Now About Drugs of Any Kind

I know that people, adults or children, don't just take drugs for no reason. They start taking drugs probably out of curiosity, but they continue using to relieve the anguish of something—to relieve a pain, a heartache, a trauma. It's a coping mechanism they have acquired because they don't have access to or knowledge of healthy coping skills. Next time you judge a so-called drug addict, take a minute and remember this. Most people are good people who don't know how to solve problems. They don't have an outlet or don't know they have other options. By the time someone notices they are struggling, they are often an addict. Change your perspective and think about this. Our bodies can, unfortunately, become victims to so many different types of illnesses, viruses or diseases. Most times, you can see them. You can see them in the physical sense of your body. You can see them on CT scans, MRI scans, X-rays, and ultrasounds. You can see it with your own eyes. You can get bloodwork done and see if your numbers are out of the typical range. We trust the reports the doctors give us because, in some way, shape or form, they SHOW us.

Mental health is a hard sickness to sell. You can't see the lack of serotonin or the fight or flight reflex that seems to be in overdrive unless you undergo extensive tests—most uncovered by insurance. You can't show someone that it is an illness when you feel like you have all the energy in the world and then weeks later have difficulty getting out of bed. When people can't SEE something to prove the illness, they have a hard time believing it. If you are one of the millions of people suffering from mental illness, I see you. You don't need to prove to anyone that something is wrong. You know your body. You know if something doesn't feel right, and, if you are unsure, there is absolutely no shame in speaking to someone who can help you identify what is going on, such as a therapist or psychiatrist. When I eventually gathered the strength to use my voice and persistence, my mom found me a psychiatrist. This was YEARS AND YEARS down the line. I used to wait until the very last appointment of the day to see my therapist. This way, it was dark enough that no one would see me get out of my car, and most likely, no one was left in the office. Out of all the things I was diagnosed with and went through, when I look back, that fact was the craziest. The fact that I felt I had to hide what I was doing sounds insane now. I was bettering myself. I was facing issues that broke my soul head-on and revisiting them week after week. I was reopening the wounds. What I was doing was hard work. What I was doing was responsible. I was ensuring I was on the way to being the best version of myself. What I should have been doing in addition to all that was BEING SEEN and telling my friends that it was okay. Looking back, what I did made me stronger than a lot of people. I wish I had been a voice for everyone parking their cars at night to get late appointments with their therapist. I wish I could have brought more attention to mental health as a whole. I wish I could've been the person people went to for advice when they were anxious, tired, lonely or lost, but I wasn't. So today, I sit here and plead with you. If you are someone who is going through this, be the voice. Be the person who makes everyone else know it's okay to be cracked. Let them know they are strong and will never be alone. Be the person I wasn't. Who knows how many lives you can change? If you are someone who is reading this and contemplating making that leap, I urge you to dive in and trust the process. Cracks are often the way that the light can find us.

If you are someone who can identify a friend or family member who may be in distress, then I beg of you, be the lifeline. I know you may feel like you can't help, but understand this: People who have experienced any kind of trauma will process things in life differently, and most likely will need a helping hand. BUT MOST IMPORTANTLY, people heal differently depending on who they surround themselves with. If you are supportive, even without understanding, you are helping to heal. If you love, without condition, you are helping to heal. If you listen without judgment, you are helping to heal. Contrary to this, if you judge, dismiss, gaslight, love but only under your conditions, then you can actually make the healing process harder, if not impossible. Choose to be the light.

My First 7

A few years ago my friend came home from a workshop on changing your mindset and exploring the characteristics in your life that define you, whether negative or positive. The conversation we had following her workshop was completely intriguing. One of the activities she spoke about and asked me to do was to write down on a piece of paper three events that stick out in your mind that occurred before age seven. I found this fascinating and, of course, had to explore this. I know that my accident would be number one, but what are the next two things that immediately pop-up in my head following that? What's crazy is that I didn't have to think very long. Two memories popped up almost instantly.

    The first memory was playing in my house with a bunch of kids. When I was younger, there was a group of adults that would get together with my parents a couple of times a month. They were our family friends. We went out to eat together, we went over each other's houses and even vacationed together. They had kids that were the same age, or close in age, to me and my brother and sister. I looked forward to the nights they would come over all the time. Me and my siblings would make lists of games we would play and snacks we would eat. We even picked out movies to watch. We would go swimming in the summertime while the parents hung out in the hot tub. The parents were always laughing and cracking jokes. We would eat outside and catch fireflies. I know that sounds cliche, but I swear we did. We would turn the hammock into a pirate ship, and one of the kids would rock the crap out of it as if we were in a storm. The last one on the hammock was the winner. After eating dinner, all the kids would go inside and play in the playroom or watch a movie in the living room. The parents would stay outside and have a couple of drinks, some dessert and maybe even play a card game.

When we went on vacation together, the parents had a saying, "Why not? We're on vacation!" That was the answer to everything we wanted. Can we get room service? "Why not? We're on vacation." Can we go down the lazy river WITHOUT the parents following us this time? "Why not? We're on vacation." If I don't eat all my dinner, can I still order dessert? "Why not? We're on vacation." Sometimes I go back and watch the old home videos, and when I come across this videotape, I immediately feel joy. Why was this memory so prominent among so many other events in my first seven years? I had no idea and would need a minute to really figure this one out.

The other memory is made up of a compilation of visuals, but also more so a feeling. When I was younger, I was loud and dramatic, and I loved to sing and put on shows. I forced my family members to sit and watch them even when, most times, they probably wanted to poke needles in their eyes! I remember my mom saying, "Come on, we have to watch her show. You know she has to be the center of attention!" I also remember my sister being about three years old, which would put me exactly at age seven. It was Christmas morning, and my sister was showing my parents her new doll. No one was paying attention to the things I got, so I jumped in front of my sister and started doing this ridiculous dance. My dad said, "Move Ella, I can't see your sister." When he saw me pouting, he said the same thing. "Okay, show us your gifts, cause god forbid it's not about Ella." They were not saying these things in a mean way. They weren't yelling or talking down to me. It was just a statement that was said in a sing-song manner as if it was something that was a matter of fact. So many times, my parents and other family members commented about me and how I had to be the center of attention. It became a joke at a certain point, that's how often they would say it. It wasn't all of this that stuck out to me though. What stuck out to me was their voice and face as they said it. They were annoyed. That's the feeling I had when I had this memory. The feeling of being annoying. So what did this all mean? I have these two prominent memories, but what do I do with them?

Jane explained to me that the next part of this process was taking the feelings from those memories and seeing how they apply to you now in the present time. Those feelings or memories, in theory, can essentially build the foundation of your characteristics or traits. They could be the building blocks that would shape your personality for the rest of your life. They could impact you in some way, but it was up to you whether you would allow the implications to be positive or negative. While I originally found this activity fascinating, now I was rather confused. What did this mean for me? Did it mean that being annoying was embedded in my personality, and that was it? Did it mean I loved vacations and gatherings with friends because they brought me joy? I started to feel like this activity was not for me. Who doesn't feel joy with friends or family or on vacation? How could I be annoying for the rest of my younger life to come if, eventually, I became invisible to my classmates and barely spoke out of fear that I would be made fun of? During college, I actually avoided being the center of attention at all costs. I HATED when people looked at me, and I especially, in no way whatsoever, would walk into a lecture hall late. Everyone would turn around as the door opened and look at you. I would actually feel like fainting. The first time it happened was the last. I felt all the blood drain from my body and my pulse like a marching band in my ears. I was going to pass out. After that, if I was late, I would take the absence. That's probably why it took me so long to graduate. In any case, how was all this correlated? This was nonsense.

What I Know Now (After Days of Self-Reflection)

This activity was actually so eye-opening and awakening! Let's tackle the easier of the two memories: being annoying. People in my family never SAID I was annoying. There were, however, implications of this when they would sigh or comment about me always having to be the center of attention. I never paid attention to this as a child, but looking back at it now through the lens of an adult, an adult who has anxiety issues, these actions, unbeknownst to them, were imprinting. THIS IS WHEN I STARTED TO FEEL SELF-CONSCIOUS. Compile this hidden emotion with what happened to me in middle and high school, and you have the perfect storm for someone who feels they have no self-worth. I was scared to speak up for myself or raise my hand in class because I thought I would be annoying. I didn't want the focus on me because, in the past, when the focus was on me, people were annoyed or bothered by me. I always went with the crowd because I didn't want to be annoying. I never said no. This is a big one. I never said no to favors, to friends' crazy ideas and the worst was I never said no when dating. I went on some dates with a lot of losers because I didn't want to say no and be talked about. I was like a puppet. Whatever anyone wanted, I did. I would rather feel uncomfortable in any situation than have people look at me with those same looks as when I was little. Those same sighs of complete annoyance. Did my family mean to do any of this? No way. However, it's like they say, kids are sponges. I subconsciously absorbed all the reactions from the people I loved every time I asked for attention. Today I am a people pleaser. I go above and beyond to help others and make people feel happy to be around me. I took what happened to me growing up, and IT IS TRUE, it shaped one of the greatest parts of my personality or character traits. One could say it affected me negatively, and some say it made me better. In one sense, I am afraid to walk into a crowded room because everyone will stare at me. I say I'm sorry at the beginning of sentences when talking to people. "I am so sorry, but can I have another napkin?" " I am sorry, but could you give me some extra help? I don't understand the lesson." "I'm sorry to bother you, but can I try on these shoes in a size seven?" I should not have to apologize for asking things of people when that is precisely what they are there to do. But I will because I don't want to be the one who annoys them that day. I couldn't even tell you the hundreds of things I did in life that I didn't actually want to do just because I didn't say no to annoy the person asking me those things.

SIDE NOTE: Some children who were exposed to narcissistic relationships will grow up to be people pleasers. So, while all these experiences made me always want to say yes to everyone, I was also around people who exhibited many characteristics of narcissism. That also played a huge role in who I became as an adult. We will talk about this more in a future chapter that focuses solely on narcissism.

On the brighter side, I am a good person. I look to make others happy so they don't find me annoying. And somewhere during this journey of making a point to be a people pleaser, I actually found joy in helping others. I will do things people ask of me today, not because I'm afraid to be annoying but because I love to help. I love to give advice, I love to physically help people and I love to be of use. Sometimes I never leave time for myself, and my husband will tell me I do too much for everyone else. But that's just it. What I do for everyone else makes me happy and makes me feel whole. It made me an empath. It gave me perspective. It gives my anxiety a sense of ease that someone else doesn't have to say "I'm sorry to ask but—" They don't have to apologize. I am there for them, any time, any day, even if they don't start with "I'm sorry to ask but—"

At the end of the day, what happened to me growing up affected me in good ways and in bad. A double-edged sword, if you will. I am a GOOD person. I help people, I try to feel how they feel and I try to see their perspective. I like to validate their feelings. The bad part? Most empaths are targets for narcissists. They can pick an empath out like a vampire finds blood!!! Many empathetic people are lucky enough to never have an intimate relationship with a narcissist. That wasn't the case for me. I had one right under my nose. I just didn't know until I was in my 30s in my own recovery. That relationship is an entire chapter within itself!

On to memory number two. This was a LOADED one psychologically and took me years to reverse. You would think fun memories of vacations and family gatherings would be a good thing to have as a kid, and it was. It's what was associated with those times that molded me. During these friends and family get-togethers and during our vacations together, the personalities of my parents shifted. They were so happy. Laughed. Smiled. Listened to each other. They told stories with enthusiasm as the friends would have tears of laughter rolling down their faces. The wives would escape and leave the men with the kids and vice versa. Whatever the reason being, they were happy. They hugged each other. They enjoyed each other. If you ask me about any other times that I can remember regarding my parents, my mind is blank. They coexisted. They worked together to pay bills and raise a family. We had Blockbuster nights with my dad in the living room, and my mom would iron from the kitchen. My mom napped a lot, which, looking back, was probably a sign of depression, and my dad worked longer and longer hours. There was no joy amongst them. There was joy in my house, don't get me wrong. But the joy was for us three kids. Not towards each other. When we went to Toys R Us, my dad would take us alone. As the years went by, we saw the family friends less and less. The kids were growing up doing their own things, my dad and brother were away at soccer tournaments on the weekends, and my mom was running errands. We weren't a family unit. As the years passed, it got even worse. At family parties, my mom would be in the kitchen with my aunts and grandmothers, and the men would sit at the table and wait to be served. We were a divided family covered in rainbows and butterflies for the world to see. My parents eventually divorced when I was in college, and it wasn't a surprise. We were, however, the first family on both my parents' sides to be divorced. I bet you're thinking this is when I talk about how divorce affected me. The crazy thing is, that's not what this memory is. The reason this memory was prominent is because it's one of the only times I can remember when we were all happy together.

So, according to this exercise, this should define me in some way… and that would be totally correct. Firstly, the distance between my parents growing up made me believe that's what marriage was. I didn't think marriage was fun. I honestly thought no matter who you married, you would eventually fall into this place where you called your best friend to complain about everything your husband did or didn't do. I thought you delegated the house chores and pooled your money together to pay bills. I thought you didn't hang out much because, eventually, the wife became a mom and the husband worked more and more. In my mind, this was marriage. This is what I, in turn, married. I married a man whom I coexisted with for the sake of doing what was the right thing to do. I am a people pleaser, right? I did what made them happy. What made my daughter happy. What made him happy. It didn't matter to me because, at the end of the day, marriages, according to my experiences, are a chore anyway. My parents didn't only set the foundation for the concept of marriage in a negative light to me. Unbeknownst to them, that memory of the family gatherings with the friends, the one where they were laughing.... is what also moved me to get a divorce. I remembered the happiness of those days, and it inspired me. It inspired me enough to ask for a divorce. It made me realize there can be happiness in a marriage. It doesn't have to be a job. I deserved to be happy. I had to break the cycle for the sake of my children. And I did. It was so hard. Gut wrenching, actually, but with the strength I never knew I had and the vivid memory of those days of happiness, I did it. I didn't know if I would find anyone to share my life with, but I did know being alone made me happier. I did know that I would be teaching my daughter not to settle. I would be teaching her to be independent and follow her heart. And maybe, just maybe, I could find someone who made me smile like that every day.

This activity made me realize that I was one of the lucky ones. I could pull out the positive from what could have been negative memories. I allowed the memories to mold me with positive characteristics or attributes rather than negative ones. This didn't come naturally, of course. It really does take a lot of work, reflection, changing your mindset, adjusting your thoughts and shifting your gratitude. I have met so many people in my life who blame their parents for their actions. "What can I do? I'm like this because my parents did this or didn't do that." While that may be true, YOU are the only person controlling your happiness and daily choices. Your parents may have done things differently or incorrectly in your eyes, but that doesn't mean you get to use that as an excuse to be anything less than the best version of yourself. Most likely, your parents, like mine, did their best. Self-reflection is huge. What do you want out of life? What do you want for yourself? What kind of people do you allow in your life? Do they hinder or help your constant evolution toward your best self? How can you be this "best version" of yourself? Don't let the curveballs of your past, the curveballs that might not even be yours, define you. You define yourself!

The Empath And The Narcissist

It wasn't always as bad as it seems
There once was a time when your arms felt like home,
and you believed in me and my dreams

A time when you listened and at least tried to care
A time when you possibly loved me, although looking back I'm not so sure you ever did,
a thought so heavy to bare

Conversations with you are often like walking through minefields, waiting for something I say or do to start the war
The arguments and disappointment is inevitable...what am I doing this all for?

A sliver of hope, a moment of your time, a glimpse of your attention at best
It all seems hopeless, exhausting on my soul and heart and I really just need to rest

All the words and promises that rolled off your tongue, big or small, all were lies
Ones that I would have seen through if I had the courage to look into your eyes

from broken to beautifully broken

So dark and empty, no warmth, or joy
The longer I stare, I can see that lost boy

A boy who grew up with so much love, yet it was never truly enough for the man who became cold and strong
who spent his whole life trying to prove others wrong

Years spent on proving his worth to people who really didn't matter
All the while leaving his family, making each day for them sadder and sadder

The days turned to weeks and weeks into years
A little girl's excitement and hope turning into disappointment and anger, resentment and tears

All the years she sat with anger it just ate at her soul never able to leave
Until one day she realized anger is the hearts way when you don't allow yourself to grieve

To mourn the loss of something you never truly had, to accept it was all a vision you held on to in your head
A realization to come to like this, can break you before you can heal, words left unspoken are now forced to be said

And all the while you played your game with guilt as your pawn
With everything the way you wanted, beautifully painted, in the picture you had drawn

But it took me breaking, starving my heart and body, tears

watering my soul through the cracks that you made
In order for all the hopes I had and visions of us to finally fade

And when the truth set in and I allowed myself to accept the things that would never be
That's when I saw what I could never see,
that's when I accepted what would never be
and that's when I realized it would be so easy for you to get over the loss of me

But I have learned your arms are not my home,
your voice doesn't calm my storms and words don't heal my heart
I am whole again and this time I won't let you break me apart

I hope someday you let someone in and you can experience the joy of others and not just the joy of yourself
I hope that one day someone is there for you and you don't know the pain of someone not wanting to help

I hope one day the gray is faded for you and you experience the brightness of the sun
And maybe then you'll realize all the things we could've done.

 I wrote that poem a few years back during therapy. It was helpful for me to get my feelings down on paper, but my god was it eye-opening. I had relationships with multiple people who carried narcissistic traits my whole life. From as far back as I can remember, I always wanted to please people. I always wanted to make them happy. I was scared to disappoint. Helping them made me feel happy. Seeing them happy because I did something for them fulfilled me. This should be the end of this chapter, right? What's wrong with pleasing people?

Absolutely nothing. There is nothing wrong with it UNLESS you are doing it as a learned behavior or a coping skill. I mentioned in the previous chapter how I felt like I was always annoying people or how my family would jokingly tell me that it had to always be "all about me." While this may have been true, everyone didn't realize the impact these words would have on me for quite some time. Ironically, being a child around someone who exhibits narcissistic traits also molded me into a people pleaser. This is simply because I used "people pleasing" as a way to stay safe and avoid conflict. I'm sure you've heard of the fight, flight or freeze response to trauma, but there is also the fawn response, which is people-pleasing. Being in any kind of relationship with a toxic person can be traumatic, and your body recognizes this threat by responding accordingly. I was also willing to jump through hoops just to get a sliver of attention from them. I can't remember much of my younger years and how they may have affected me, but I can remember the EXACT moment the light bulb went off that there were some red flags around me.

It was my birthday, and I had family coming over. My father decided this would be the day he would leave our home, our family, my mom and his three kids. We knew that our parents were divorcing, as they had set us down and had a conversation about it. What we didn't know was the exact moment he was leaving. The family came over to celebrate, and we were left explaining why my dad was gone. The day was ruined. People smiled while hiding their sorrow from us. We sang happy birthday, and the pictures from that day are all stained with swollen red eyes. Was it necessary for him to leave at that moment? No. Was it necessary TO HIM to leave in that moment? Probably. I truly feel he was probably uncomfortable and he just wanted out. He didn't want to explain himself. He didn't want to engage with family and pretend it was all fine. He wanted out and that's all that seemed to matter. To be honest, if I were in his shoes, I really wouldn't want to sit around a house full of people and be questioned about my divorce either. However, what bothers me is that it felt like he didn't care whose heart broke or the lasting emotional scars this would have on his then wife and kids if he left THAT day. He seemed to care more about what it would be like for him to be there that day than what it would feel like for all of us. For about ten years I tried to understand why my dad would want to leave on such a special day, but it wasn't until I understood mental health, narcissistic characteristics, and emotional intelligence that it made sense. Once I could finally interpret his behaviors in this memory ingrained in my mind, I could see the memory much clearer. Unfortunately, so many red flags also popped up in my head, which was extremely overwhelming. To have insight like this can be difficult to process. Especially if these moments all flood your brain at once, especially if it was in regard to many people you once or still love.

I remember a time I found out my boyfriend was cheating on me. I came home crying hysterically, and my dad called my grandmother. She came over, and the two of them yelled at me for crying. They told me I was stronger than that. "We" don't cry over losers. My grandmother called him a cockroach and told me I was better than this. Better than what? Showing my emotion? Here's the thing. I was raised to think showing your emotion was a weakness. If I cried over a "cockroach" what did that make me? So here we have two very big red flags that went unnoticed until I was a bit older. One...What he wanted was all that seemed to matter in my eyes. His appearance and wants seemed to be more important than the feelings of those he supposedly cared about. Two… I wasn't supposed to feel my emotions. I wasn't supposed to express myself. I was taught that, but my father was ALSO taught that growing up. My feelings felt completely invalidated.

Red flag three. These men that had been in my life at one point or another ESPECIALLY didn't like me to express myself when it came to conflicting opinions of their own. If I mentioned something that bothered me or something that was upsetting me, or something I felt

from broken to beautifully broken

was unfair, I was completely shut down. If those feelings didn't align with theirs, they were wrong. They were invalidated, they were incorrect, and GET THIS... the narrative of the story was changed so that my feelings couldn't be validated. They could in no way be true if the story changed. For the greater part of the conversations, I would be convinced that the way they told the story was correct, and therefore my feelings were unjust. I spent years and years trying to get my point of view to be seen. I just wanted them to see why so many things they did or didn't do hurt me. But whenever I opened my mouth, it always ended the same way. Not speaking for long periods of time, possibly even months. It was like once I spoke up and proved my point, one of two things happened. One: I was convinced I was wrong in my feelings, and two: if that didn't work, a reason was found to hang up the phone, walk away or end the conversation, and I didn't hear back for months. Literally months. These people would rather distance themselves from me and miss out on my life than simply apologize or admit what they did was wrong and then work on it for the future. This act of self-reflection and change NEVER happened on any of their parts. Even as I write this. Their way was the only way, and if I couldn't see that, I was cut off. One person in particular had exact words they ALWAYS said to me, "El, you got it all wrong."

Since my 30s began, my relationship with my dad had unfortunately become less and less. This was not my choice. He remarried (or at least I think he did, and if he did I wasn't there), and he raised two step-children with his wife. I saw him once a year for Christmas Eve until that stopped and once a year for Father's Day until that stopped as well. When we all did get together, the same stories were spoken at dinner.

1. My sister was a genomic scientist and a genius. We always talked about her success, and rightfully so. She really was so smart and deserved to celebrate all her accomplishments. My

dad made sure to vocalize his extreme pride in her every time we all got together.
2. Whatever project my dad was working on. He had to show us pictures of his accomplishments and show us how much better of a man he is now in life, and sometimes it even felt to me like he was showing how much more successful he was than any of us.
3. Sports. He and my brother always bonded over soccer, and most times, we went places where there was a bar and a television to watch some kind of game. My brother had a good relationship with them because they shared a love of soccer.
4. My teenage years. We ALWAYS, ALWAYS had to talk about the things I did to get in trouble as a teenager. He always said the same phrase: "El was my hardest kid. She was always in trouble." While this may have been true, it would've probably been to his benefit to figure out why I was always in trouble. Also, as a side note, my siblings got in the same trouble. I just covered for them and taught them what NOT to do to get caught.

These family outings became increasingly undesirable to me as I began to identify the red flags. Most of the time, my dad would pick a spot to get together that would not be appropriate for children. I had two small kids. He would either choose a bar-type restaurant or an extremely late dinner time. He would choose places requiring you to park in a parking garage and walk a few blocks, or places with loud music and chaos. All of which made it extremely difficult for me to participate. I would ask to change the location, but if I did, he would tell me it isn't just about me. This enraged me every time, but I couldn't find a way to make him understand that it wasn't about what I wanted; it was about what everyone would be able to participate in comfortably and that I, unfortunately, would have to turn down the

from broken to beautifully broken

invite if it was inappropriate for my children. The next year would roll around, and I knew we were approaching when I would see my dad again.

I thought if I were proactive, it would make this a little easier. I offered to host the dinners at my house. I would have it catered or barbecue, have the bar stocked with everyone's favorite drinks, music, backyard games...whatever anyone wanted. It would be a lot of work, but my kids had their bedrooms a few feet away and could go to sleep at a normal time. They also wouldn't have to walk four blocks with their little legs, or go to a place with a loud atmosphere. Every single time I offered, my dad would say it sounded nice and would check with everyone and see when it got closer. Well, as you probably assumed already, the time would get closer, and the text would get sent out about going out. My dad would start the conversation by saying he assumed no one planned anything for Father's Day, so he picked the place. (insert one of the above inappropriate-for-children places). When I would remind him that I offered to host, he would say he either forgot, or "No I like to go out, it's easier," or the BEST was, "It's just too much work for you." As if any of the other places were less work for me! This is another red flag I didn't learn about until I had wasted so many tears and arguments. My dad really only did the things HE WANTED TO DO. He wanted us to always show up when he wanted but rarely showed up for the things I asked him to show up for. Sure, he was lots of fun, but only if it was something he enjoyed. He didn't waste time doing things that didn't interest or benefit him.

At a certain point, I had to talk with my dad. I was always so scared to use my voice with him, and I didn't know why. I just knew when I had conversations with him, it was extremely emotional for me, so when I finally had enough and had to have a conversation, it meant I was really hurting. It had been a while since I saw my dad. Like I said, these outings were too much with two kids. They didn't take into account my children, and so I had to slowly stop going. In reality, I wasn't rushing to a dinner where I was the "bad kid" anyway. I was okay with not seeing him often—I was used to it. The thing is, I wanted my kids to have memories with their grandfather. It had been almost a year at this point that we had seen him. So I dialed his number and started this god-awful conversation. I told him I didn't understand how he didn't WANT to see his grandkids. I told him all we really want is his time and attention, and I asked why that was so hard. After a plethora of excuses including work and not wanting to be with my mother, none of which included accountability or even a sign that he felt sorry that it was this way, he referred to his girlfriend as his wife in one of his sentences. I stopped dead in my thoughts because not only did it feel like my dad did not want anything to do with me or my kids, but he never even invited us to his wedding?! I had no idea at what point the transition from girlfriend to wife took place. I was so hurt and offended. I felt like I didn't matter at all. What the actual hell was going on?

"She's your wife? Since when?" came right out of my mouth without hesitation. My father took that comment as disrespectful, and just like that, everything I had been upset over became irrelevant. It was like my concerns had just disappeared. The only thing that mattered were those two small sentences I said. The rest of the conversation was out the window. All the courage it took to talk about what bothered me did not even matter. All that mattered was I asked a question he didn't want to answer and then used that as his gateway to flip the narrative and make me the reason he has not been around for the next year. We didn't talk for a very long time after that. No calls. No texts. Nothing. He missed my son's christening. NOT because he wasn't invited but because—again, being an empath—I did the right thing and sent an invitation WITH a follow-up text regarding the christening. He didn't even RSVP to the invite or respond to the text. He could just stop a conversation when he didn't like it and never turn back. He either stopped calling or stopped responding. He would even blameshift trying to make himself the victim and then use that reason to never call again or resolve the issue. He would much rather lose me than be at fault. My question to him was not rude. It was a real question. Honestly, it was a question I didn't even know I wanted the answer to. Because his answer might have actually meant that he cut me out of something so important in his life. He used that against me. He used that as a way to silence me from all the other stuff I wanted to address. He used that to avoid me for months.

My dad and I finally reconnected a day before I had to have major surgery. My aunt called him and told him I was having this surgery. He called me and told me, all differences aside, I'm still his daughter, and he wanted to make sure I was okay. For the record, I felt like he was calling because, in his own selfish way, if something happened to me, he couldn't live with the fact that we hadn't talked. But even in my mid 30s, the little girl in me really, really was hoping he actually cared. This kind of relationship continued up until just a short while ago. After being in treatment for an eating disorder, I finally realized my self-worth and my relationship with him had changed vastly. Four months of being in a hospital, six hours of therapy daily and I finally have a sliver of the realization and perspective I needed. So, life threw me a handful of narcissists, and I didn't do too well with that.

What I Know Now

It is true that if you love a narcissist, you will often go to extreme lengths to get their attention or approval. You'll even beg for just one simple compliment. This is not a defect of your personality. This is a conditioned response. You are not desperate. You are not worthless. Your value is not contingent upon them. You probably don't even know what exactly you want in life anymore because this person has already embedded their wants as YOUR WANTS. It's a constant, vicious cycle of "Hey, look what I did," and the response being nothing. This completely invalidates your efforts giving you a lower sense of self-worth, which in turn snowballs into many possible serious mental illnesses. We have low self-esteem, codependency, anxiety, depression and eating disorders… just to name a few.

When my dad left on my 21st birthday, I would tell myself that it had absolutely nothing to do with me. It had to do with the fact that he had his own insecurities about that day, and he only thought about his feelings. He was more concerned about how he looked in everyone else's eyes or how he felt uncomfortable more than anyone else around him. That's not me being worthless or of no value. It was about him. My dad leaving was about the issues he was having in his life. They were not a reflection of me and my worth. When he left, it seemed like he was not protecting me or my feelings. For years my self-worth plummeted, and I had no idea that part of it may have stemmed from this.

Contrary to my own thought, it DID NOT mean I wasn't worth protecting. According to author Ally Wise, *"One of our three foundational needs as a human is safety. If that need goes unmet our perception of ourselves becomes altered and we are in a constant state of survival mode."* Being in survival mode year after year actually made my body sick. It affected my mind and my decision making, and I was truly sick. For years my anxiety was complicated by the fact that I felt like I didn't have anyone to actually count on to protect me. When that boyfriend cheated on me (again, I had no sense of self-worth) and I cried and showed my raw emotion, I was immediately scolded. Expressing myself in any capacity that made me look weak was frowned upon. I was supposed to just listen and do as they like, feel as they say. But if I could turn back time, I would tell my younger self to LET IT OUT. Feel the heartache. Feel the betrayal. Feel the insecurity. Feel it all. These experiences shape us and help us process emotions healthily as we grow older. Bottling up emotions never had a good outcome. Those emotions grow like cancer on your soul until we are unable to control them any longer. Being emotionless or "strong" doesn't make you a better person. What if you simply don't want to be "strong?" What if you want to experience your feelings and understand them so that in the future, you know how to control them in a healthy way?

As I got older, I began finding the little bit of courage I had to use my voice and speak about the things that bothered me. As you already know, this went sideways every single time. I needed to step outside of the conversation or argument and gain perspective. I had to recall what I knew and learned about emotional intelligence. Is this person capable of living up to my expectations in the first place? Is this person emotionally capable of understanding anyone's feelings besides their own? What I really SHOULD have done was NOTHING! It is not my job to teach a grown person what they are doing right and wrong in life. It's not my job to explain to them how their actions are hurtful. It is not my job to protect their emotions or ego. I should have just let them be. Let them exist as they please, and then I CAN DECIDE whether or not their true personality is one I want in my life. I CAN create that boundary, and if they don't like it, then I can confirm that they indeed need that boundary. You can not control anyone's responses or emotions. What you can do is control how you respond to them. That is in your control. That ball is in your court. Don't pass that ball!

If there is any message you take away from this chapter, let it be this. No matter what your story is, no matter what your feelings are, no matter if you beg or plead, a narcissist will never take accountability. They will blameshift and gaslight you, and they are always a hero in their own story. Once you no longer serve a purpose and are unable to be manipulated, they will become the victim in the story where they have you as the villain. This is probably very hard to understand now if you are at the beginning of your healing journey, but please believe that there is a point where a victim of narcissism will become enlightened. The light bulb goes off, and you start to undo all the things that were ingrained in your mind by them. You'll start with self-awareness, and eventually you will have self-love. It takes time. It takes work. It takes digging into the places that are raw and still aching. It's not fun, but it is so damn liberating to finally feel like you've stepped out of this vortex of lies and manipulation. Remember this: if you are an empath, you will naturally give another person a safe space where they can express themselves. You will even try to see things from their perspective to understand them better. However, just because they have wounds that hurt them, it does not give them the right to hurt you. You can give them the space they need with you while also maintaining boundaries to protect yourself from being their target. Only take on what you are comfortable with and trust your journey (and your gut).

The Rabbit Hole

As a little girl, I watched all the princess movies. I dressed up like a princess and sang the songs from *The Little Mermaid* with my whole heart and soul… still do. I waited my whole life to be "rescued" by a prince. I yearned for the feeling of love at first sight. As a young adult, I believed in soulmates. I believed that there really was one person that was chosen for me and we would eventually cross paths at the right time and end up together forever. I was a hopeless romantic, blinded by the thoughts of happily ever after. It sounds strange because the house I was brought up in was the complete opposite. Maybe that's why I was so drawn to the thought of it. Maybe I wanted to prove that marriage was a good thing. Maybe I just wanted to live in a fairy tale to escape my everyday life filled with anxious thoughts and a boyfriend who taught me there is a thin line between love and hate. What I wished for was a Prince Charming, and what I got was the opposite of a fairytale. I went from yearning for *love at first sight* to *love is blind* real quick. I had just graduated high school when I met Nate.

The relationship I had with Nate was complicated from day one. When we first were introduced to each other, I had a boyfriend of two years. My boyfriend lied to me, cheated on me and abused me emotionally and sometimes physically. I was scared that if I left him, I would never have another boyfriend. I thought people would see the old me, and he made sure to let me know that most guys wouldn't date a girl with a scar on her face. He pushed me out of his car as he was pulling out of the driveway and left me there. He snuck out at night to see other girls. He was a liar and god only knows what else. Eventually, he broke into my house while my family and I were on vacation, took my car out of the garage with the spare key I left at his house and picked up the girl he was cheating on me with. You could only imagine the vision of my parents losing their shit when we pulled up to our house to see a hole in our garage door and my car covered in snow from being driven. After that episode, we were heading toward the end of our relationship for many reasons, but once I started college, we broke up shortly after for good. I find it important to speak of that relationship before I get into Nate for a reason. When you are with someone who treats you so poorly, the man in your next relationship really has to show just the slightest form of affection for you to automatically become entranced. Any man after a relationship like that was a step up! It's like breathing fresh air after sucking down poison for two years.

Nate was always around because we were in the same friendship group. Whenever we went out as a group to a party, to a club, wherever… he was there. He was the type of guy that the girls whispered about as he passed. The attention seeker. Everywhere this guy went, girls would stare. I was curious about him, but I also just got out of a very abusive relationship, and I was emotionally and mentally damaged. I had to work through what had happened in my last relationship in order to be in a healthy relationship in the future, but if you've been reading any of this book, you know my level of anxiety and can probably guess that my plethora of issues kept me from doing any of that. The easiest way to distract yourself from a breakup was a rebound. At least, I thought that's what it would be. What our relationship became was more emotionally abusive than anything I had ever experienced before. Nate wanted to "date" me but only under his conditions. He didn't want anything serious, and that was fine with me… at first. I wanted to explore the dating world just as much, so the

from broken to beautifully broken

occasional hookup with Nate fit perfectly into my new lifestyle. Slowly we started seeing each other more and more, and what was a casual thing became me actually caring about him. When we were all together, his friends would tease him, saying they knew he liked me but wouldn't admit it. His response always was, "Not me, we're just friends." He always told everyone we were just friends. We would go out, and he would hook up with other girls in front of me but then ask me to sleep over. We went to the Bahamas as a group of about 20 people. He hooked up with girls every single day, sometimes three feet away from me. The moment I started having a CONVERSATION with another boy, he called me a slut. What Nate ultimately wanted was to have his cake and eat it too. He wanted me when he wanted me, and when he didn't, I had to sit and wait around like a lost puppy without him. My lack of self-esteem, coupled with the lack of a therapist and my abusive previous relationship was a perfect storm for me to actually listen to him. I stopped talking to other guys. I stopped going out without him. Nate kept doing what he did best—dating a different girl every week and calling me at night. I couldn't understand why I wasn't enough. I started to buy him things thinking his love could be bought. I thought if I got him nice things, he would see how much I cared. Nope. What started happening was Nate started ASKING FOR MORE THINGS. Whenever he wanted something, he would hang out with me for a few days in a row without seeing anyone else and then turn on the charm as he nonchalantly mentioned an item he wanted. I bought it like a sucker. I hate who I was, and this particular chapter is the hardest for me to write. It's the hardest because I was the most naive, desperate human who allowed a man to take full advantage of her, EVEN if, in the back of her mind, she was fully aware that was happening.

When gifts were not enough anymore, I started paying for dinners and drinks when we went out. When dinners and drinks weren't enough, I would help him with schoolwork. Actually, let me go back and restate that. I would DO his schoolwork. Papers, online quizzes, you name it, while he would leave me in his room to go to the gym, tanning, or get a car wash. I'm going to say this again so it sinks in how low my self-esteem and self-worth was. I would sit in Nate's room and WRITE HIS PAPERS while he went out. Sometimes they took me hours. I didn't care because it was something that would allow me to see him and eventually hang out with him. Also, in my mind, he would appreciate me, and helping him would make him happy. I still had issues saying no to people for fear of rejection or that look of annoyance.

He was bread-crumbing me, and I ate every last piece. He gave me the bare minimum. Just enough to keep me around but not enough to show any commitment. He gave me just enough not to starve but never enough to feel full. Eventually, something happened that I never expected. Nate wanted a relationship. After years of bullshit. After years of stringing me along and me trying everything I could to get his attention, he finally decided he wanted to be with me and only me. I know you're all waiting for me to say it was all worth it in the end. WRONG. NO. NOT THIS CHAPTER. NOT THIS STORY. Being in a relationship with Nate meant allowing him to control me completely. He told me where I could go, when I could go, what I could wear and what I couldn't. He told me who I could talk to and who I could be friends with, and if I did anything questionable to him, I found myself under a complete interrogation and an irate boyfriend. Do you want to know what would happen after Nate accused me of doing something I didn't do? He would yell and call me names, but when he was done, he would tell me he was going out with our friends and he didn't want me there. He made himself the victim, and I suddenly needed to be punished. He would go to clubs where all my girlfriends would be, and he would make me stay home. He got a shore house with a group of guys, and I wasn't allowed to go! Every weekend he would go to the shore, and every weekend I would stay home. I

from broken to beautifully broken

knew everyone anyway, but I was so scared to defy him. The things he would say or do after were so mean. If I did something he specifically told me not to do, he wouldn't answer my call for days. I would have no idea where he was unless one of my friends told me. My anxiety level when he wouldn't answer my calls was insane. It was a downward spiral to literally acting insane. When he felt like I had been punished enough, he would call back and things would go back to how we were. We must have broken up 100 times, each time chipping a little more away from me. It took one specific incident for me to finally, completely crack. I get hives when I think of it.

    I had a lot of people in my life that I was friendly with but were not my people. Some of them were old friends from high school, some were friends of friends, but I knew a lot of people, and all of those people knew I was Nate's girlfriend. One of my friends from high school, who I was not very close with any longer, lived down the street from Nate. They went to the same college, and sometimes Nate would pick her and another girl up to go to classes together. I was with Nate for a few years at this point, and I had known this girl since high school. I started to suspect something was up when I saw her calling more frequently. He would try to hide the calls, but I saw. On the nights he didn't want to hang out, I would drive around and see if I could find him. Something in my gut told me this wasn't right. It took months of me searching his room, driving past his house and looking through his phone like a lunatic until I finally saw it with my own two eyes. Nate had told me he was tired and staying at home to sleep. I got in my car and drove past his house. As I approached the house, I saw a car parked in front of the mailbox. My heart was pounding. I couldn't even swallow. It was her car. I called Nate from my Nextel and he didn't answer. He was sleeping, right? I left him a message that, to this day, I still can't remember. I don't know what I said or if I even made sense because I was just spewing words of rage. The next day I called this girl and asked her to be very honest with me. I asked her to tell me what was going on with Nate. Never in a million years did I expect this answer.

"Nate told me you might do this," she said.

"I'm sorry, do what exactly?"

"Obsess over him still."

I saw black. My hands shook, and I thought I was going to faint. What in the actual hell was she talking about?!

"I don't understand what you're talking about."

She continued the conversation saying she knew that I was together with Nate for a long time, but that I had to stop calling him and let them have their relationship now.

"Your relationship? I'm still dating him. I was just with him two nights ago! Do you want me to call him right now and prove that to you? He is cheating on me and lying to you to make me look crazy!"

She told me she actually just spoke to him, and he gave her a heads up that I was spiraling, so she expected my call. He warned her a long time ago that if she saw my car at his house, it was because I would randomly stop there to convince him to get back together. She continued, saying I called him all the time when she's with him and he doesn't answer. She didn't understand why I didn't get that he just didn't want to be with me anymore.

"That's it. I'm coming to your house. Come outside, I'm calling him on speaker, and you can see we are still dating."

On the car ride to her house, I felt my whole world crumbling. Once I arrived, she came outside. She looked at me with pity. I called Nate on speaker. He answered. I would finally be able to prove I wasn't the things he said and that he had made up this strategic plan to trick us both.

"Hey, Nate. I'm gonna come over in a little while so we can talk about this. Are you home?" I knew when he answered it would be enough to prove that he WELCOMED my visits cause we were STILL TOGETHER.

He told me to stop calling, and that enough was enough. He knew I was with her.

I had officially entered the twilight zone. Do you know what it feels like for someone to make you into something you're not? Especially when they are trying to paint a picture of you as desperate and delusional. I asked her to get out of my car, and I went home. I was defeated and dumbfounded, and this crack was DEEP. All of her friends were talking about me. Their whispers brought me back to elementary school, and I knew I was headed to a bad place mentally. There is no turn in the story here. I went home, and Nate continued dating her. He was with me for four years and he ended our relationship for her in a dishonest, cowardly way, and it left me in a dark place.

I drank a lot and took anxiety medication. One night I drank a glass of wine in my bedroom in the basement of my mom's house. My anxiety was rising, and I was close to a full-blown panic attack. I took too much Xanax, and my stomach was burning. I crawled up the stairs, barely able to walk. I just needed to get to the bathroom before I threw up. I couldn't make it. It took all the energy I had, but somehow I was able to call my mom's name loud enough for her to hear me, then I passed out. Shortly after, I could hear everything happening around me, but I couldn't respond in any way possible. I couldn't move my body, speak or even flicker an eye open and closed. My sister sat next to me, screaming, "What did you do? What did you take?" She kept smacking my face and screaming while mom just kept yelling my name. I kept willing myself to snap out of it. I needed to wake up, I needed to reverse the events of this night. Suddenly, I took a huge gasp of breath and was able to open my eyes. I guess you can say I overdosed on medication or that mixing it with alcohol made the medications dangerous. Was I trying to kill myself again? I don't think so. I really don't. I think that I needed a way to disappear from reality for a little bit, and the only way I knew how to do this was with some kind of substance. I still didn't seek the mental help I needed because I was ultimately in denial or embarrassed to ask. Part of the reason, or most of the reason I wrote this book, was to make sure that the person holding this book in their hands knows that it is okay to ask for help. It's okay to feel like there are no other options, but it's not okay to ignore that feeling. You need to act on it immediately by finding the right avenue of mental health help. Substance abuse, attempting suicide, denial, running from the truth… those things will only get worse. So if there's one thing you can take from this book, it's to please use mental health professionals to help you. It is the most responsible, courageous thing you can do for yourself.

After this episode, I decided I needed to move on with my life to better things. Nate would not determine my destiny. I started hanging out with friends more. The confidence that was stripped away from me started resurfacing. As soon as I felt like my life was finally resembling some sort of freedom, Nate showed up at my door.

It had been a few months, and seeing his face brought so many emotions that I wanted to just push down deep and run from. Instead, I let him talk as if he even deserved that right. He told me he had made a mistake and this girl wasn't the same as what we had. In a weird way, it felt like I had won. In this moment, with those words, I could prove to everyone I was right and I wasn't crazy. I didn't immediately let Nate back into my life, but he inched his way in little by little. I was not all in, but I knew that I would be eventually. What came next was ultimately the reason he and I could never work out despite years of counseling down the line.

It was November, and my period was late. I was 22. I was still getting my degree in psychology and teaching. I was close to finishing, but not close enough yet. I showed up at Nate's house with a positive pregnancy test. His reaction was disbelief at first, but almost immediately, he became happy. He was positive that he wanted to have this baby, and here I was still trying to figure out if I truly could love him the way I did before he cheated on me and made me look unhinged. Nate told his mother, who, to my surprise, was ecstatic! She even offered to move me in and help raise the baby so I could finish school. I always loved children. I played with dolls until I was 12, and when I was little I would pray they would "come alive." I wrote my essay in college on anti-abortion, and I even wore one of those little feet pins on my jean jacket that promoted anti-abortion. I was going to school to work with kids, and I loved babies. I guess we were doing this. Eventually, I would be able to move on from the deception and hurt, and now that we were having a baby, we had so much to bring us closer together. The next step was to tell my parents.

My parents were divorced at this point, but it was only for about a year. At that time, they still communicated with one another when it came to the three children they had together. I went home to my mother's house and asked her to tell my dad to come over. She instantly knew this had to be bad. My parents spoke, but to ask him to step foot in the house was a BIG ASK. It had to be this way because the fear of telling them was absurd. I could not tell them twice. No way. They had to be there together. When my dad got there, he never even sat down. My anxiety level skyrocketed, but this time I couldn't take something to mentally disappear. I had to just let it out. I told them I was pregnant and we were going to have the baby. My mother looked sad. My dad was stone faced. He spoke first.

"No."

"Ummm. No?"

I sat in silence. Was he right? My dad typically only made decisions that benefited him, so was his advice genuine, or did he want to save himself the embarrassment when HIS friends and family found out and started talking? My mom was worried. She asked how I would be able to do this. How would I finish school? How could I afford it? How can I give this baby its best life? I left the house sad, confused and torn. My parents did not support me. They didn't want anything to do with it.

Nate and I decided I would move in with him and his mom and we would do this! We told all of our friends, and the word spread quickly. I was ten weeks pregnant when Nate told me he changed his mind. I don't know why. I don't know when he started contemplating it, but we had already told everyone. We had a plan! He told me he didn't want to have a baby at such a young age and wasn't ready. With that being said, I had no support. I had nowhere to live, no one to help me. In hindsight, I am sure my mother would have loved to help but couldn't. She had just gotten divorced, sold our beautiful house to downsize to a townhouse, and she was struggling financially. She was still teaching, so how could she actually help? Nate and other family members convinced me that the most responsible thing to do would be to terminate the pregnancy. So that's what I did. That's what I DID ALONE. This was something I thought Nate would hold my hand through, but instead, he told me that he didn't believe in abortions and couldn't be there when it happened. It was too much for him.

"So let me understand this better. You don't want anything to do with having a baby, but you also don't want anything to do with the abortion? Because it's too much for YOU to handle?"

Nate didn't even answer me. He walked inside his house, and I went home to my mom. She called our doctor, and he recommended somewhere we could go.

I still remember what I was wearing that day. I remember the terry cloth jumpsuit I wore as I walked through picketers screaming at me and spitting at my feet. I remember the people outside showing me pictures of what my baby looked like and screaming at me that I was killing an American baby. I remember the bright purple waiting room filled with women of all ages. I remember seeing a mother there with her children waiting to be called in while her husband watched their kids in the waiting room. I saw girls years younger than me, and I wanted to run. I wanted to run out of that building and disappear from everyone. Just as the room began to spiral, they called my name.

from broken to beautifully broken

My mom waited for me as I was herded into a room with about ten other girls. They gave us yellow paper gowns to wear and sat us in a circle in what looked like a basement room. We were called one-by-one into another room for an ultrasound. They turned the screen so I couldn't see, but when they printed the picture of the baby, they left it in plain sight for me. I went numb. The rest of this journey was me going through the motions, but I was not mentally present. I think my body went into fight or flight mode, and the only way I could handle this was disassociation. I remember the burning in my arms and chest as they injected me with anesthesia. I remember tasting onions, and then I remember waking up on a stretcher in a hallway. There was a bag with my clothes in it and another bag that was my "goodie bag." It had all the prescriptions I needed, along with some written instructions. No more than five minutes after I opened my eyes, they told me to get dressed. I was finished and could go. I could not even stand up straight yet, but I somehow managed to get my clothes on and make it to my mom. She helped me walk to the front door and went to get the car so that I didn't have to walk through that crowd of picketers again.

Nate visited after, but I am pretty sure I was still in denial. I remember going into the bathroom and praying that I was one of the few girls that an abortion didn't work on. I prayed there would be no blood, but no such luck. I remember wanting to go to bed, and I asked everyone to leave me. This right here is the reason Nate and I never stood a chance. I had already harbored anger and resentment from what he previously did to me, and now he blindsided me AGAIN. The resentment boiled over with his lack of support and not giving a crap about how I would feel going through this alone. Why did he get to protect himself from the engrained vision I will forever have when HE was the one who wanted this? When everyone found out I was no longer pregnant, I had to deal with all sorts of rumors spreading. Everyone speculated that I had a miscarriage or abortion. I didn't confirm or deny any of it. The last thing I could handle was judgment and having to rehash this story time after time. This didn't crack me or leave a little chip. This broke me.

After 22 years, I finally saw a psychiatrist and a therapist. I was prescribed medications for depression and anxiety, and I went to my therapist twice a week. It helped a lot. I could express myself to someone who didn't have an opinion of me. I was heard and offered support, and I became stronger. After a few months, I knew Nate was not my person. Someone who has hurt you over and over again in such deep ways could never be your person. We broke up, and I started dating someone else. He was kind, respectful and he treated me unlike anyone had before. I liked him, but I also didn't feel a spark with him. I needed to get away with my girls and clear my head. My best friends took me to Vegas for a long weekend. While I was there, he called and checked up on me, sent me cute texts and told me he missed me a million times. The last night I was there, I came home to our hotel room to find flowers at my door. I thought it was a bit excessive on his part. I just wanted a few days away with my friends, and he had to keep making his presence known! I opened the card, and my jaw dropped. They were from Nate.

He was trying to charm his way back in again, but he also hated that I was talking to someone new and was happy without him. He hated that I was in Vegas with my girls, and he needed my attention. I called him to thank him for the flowers and when he answered he explained he was in the hospital getting emergency surgery. My friends didn't buy it. They believed he was getting surgery, but they believed the motive behind the flowers was to get me to call so that he could tell me about the surgery, which then would lure me back in. It was only a few months, so they didn't think I was strong enough or had the self-confidence I needed to completely move on, even though I was truly trying in therapy. They were right. When I got home, I ended my relationship with the new guy I was dating. I just didn't feel right, and

I didn't want to string him along. I visited Nate, and he swore he was changing. He swore he wanted to be a better man for me. My naive, damaged inner child believed him, but I still couldn't unload all my resentment toward him. I had to figure out how to get past everything he did. People can change. People can be sorry. I thought, with therapy, I could work on this, and with him proving he would treat me better, we could get to a good place together. I was heading down the same rabbit hole.

One month into us slowly talking again, I was pregnant again. My mother told me she knew it would happen. She thought because I took the abortion so harshly, the only thing that would pull me out of the regret would be to have another baby. I did not plan this pregnancy. I wasn't even sure Nate and I were "fixed." My friends think Nate did it to ensure I wouldn't leave him. All I knew was no one would tell me what to do with my body or my baby again. Nate proposed to me when I was five months pregnant, and I didn't feel the things I expected to feel my whole life when I became engaged. It was almost like I knew this was the next step, and no matter how I felt about my resentment, I had to make this work for my daughter. She deserved a mother and father who lived together, and with Nate finally showing me respect, it would only be a matter of time before I would get over the past. Love doesn't just disappear, right?

What I Know Now

I didn't need Prince Charming! I didn't need rescuing. This childhood mentality is what got me all twisted in the first place. Why do we teach our children that a man needs to save us? That a woman is only whole once she becomes attached to a man? Why do we put such emphasis on marriage and having children? Why aren't we teaching our girls that YOU ARE YOUR OWN HERO? We need to teach our girls that they make themselves complete with their own needs and desires. I want my daughter to know she is enough, period. A man is a wonderful ADDITION to your aspirations, but he is not your entire dream. A man holds no power over you and vice versa. I wish I would have had enough self-confidence to remove myself from both of my boyfriends who didn't treat me with respect. When everyone in town found out I was pregnant with my daughter, they all talked about me. They all whispered how I could never do it, how the child wouldn't have a good life, and how my parents let me ruin my life. I spent the greater part of my daughter's life trying to prove those people wrong. Those people were irrelevant, and I gave them so much of my focus and energy. I never allowed anyone to help me with my daughter simply because I had to PROVE THEM WRONG. Who did that end up hurting? Not them, me! Growing up, I went through a lot of things that caused certain behaviors. The bullying caused low self-esteem and low self-worth. Being raised around narcissists made me a people pleaser and unable to say no for fear of judgment. My unaddressed mental health issues put me in positions where I used substances to calm my mind. In doing so, I made awful decisions in my relationships. Being raised in a home that made marriage feel like an obligation, where love was not the focus, made me copycat those relationships. Can I blame all of these things on why I stayed with two men who were either physically or emotionally abusive? Probably, but while those men did what they did, I need to take accountability and understand why I stayed and allowed that. Firstly, I didn't get the mental health I needed. If I had, I probably wouldn't have ended up in the position I did. If I had listened to my heart and made my own boundaries, I could've possibly avoided an abortion. But what is the use of sitting here and saying WHAT IF or I COULD HAVE? Instead, I need to understand what to do with this experience. I need to reflect on what life was teaching me and how I could use this to help me in the future.

After being treated so poorly for so long, I knew what I wanted in my next relationship. I knew what was acceptable behavior and what I would not put up with. I knew what my deal breakers were and what I deserved from a relationship. I learned to give myself grace, because how could I learn from the awful mistakes if I didn't sit with the anger and grief for a bit? I needed to truly process. I learned love can't be bought and that, for the most part, a zebra doesn't change its stripes. Nate showed his true self to me from day one. I chose to believe I could change him into someone I wanted him to be. He was his authentic self, and I didn't want to see that. That's on me.

I learned that no one can do anything to you that you don't allow. After reflecting on my personal relationships, I realize I was already broken before meeting either of them. The only reason they could take such advantage of me was because I was broken. Most of the time, people who are abused in relationships are already traumatized by something previous in their lives, allowing them to accept their partner's behaviors. Something from the past is haunting them, and they need to dig deep and figure that out.

I learned that you don't always need to tell your side of the story. People will talk about you. People will talk about what they THINK they know about you, and you need to decide whether it's worth your time or not to defend your character. Because at the end of the day, the truth always comes out. So, if people want to talk, let them talk. You don't always have to answer. Sometimes it's more important to protect your own mental health than to prove to somebody else, who has no significance in your life, your side of the story.

I learned that it is never okay for anyone to hurt me, whether it be my self-esteem or physically, emotionally or mentally. I have to be okay with walking away from a relationship that does that, knowing that I am much better off by myself. Which brings me to another thing I realized. I had to learn to sit and love myself without anyone's help. I needed to know that I was okay being in a relationship with myself. I needed to know that I could make myself happy and I didn't have to depend on anybody else for that happiness. And once I was okay with being my own true source of happiness, I finally got into a healthy relationship (which I talk about in the chapter titled, *It Only Took 13 Years.*) If you don't love yourself, how can you expect anyone else to love you the way you deserve?

Most importantly, I learned that forgiveness is not an easy pill to swallow but a necessary one. I forgave Nate and my boyfriend before him. I did not condone their actions, nor will I forget them. But holding onto such hate and anger will only poison me. I needed to let it go, and forgive them, without an apology, for not knowing better. They were young, and we all make mistakes. Mostly, I needed to forgive my younger self for allowing those things in my life, and once forgiveness was attainable on all ends, I started to feel a little less broken.

The Empty Casket

I was able to graduate college with my degree in psychology and my teaching license just in time. My daughter was born on my college graduation day. When my daughter was born, we lived with Nate's mom for about one year. She helped us take care of our daughter and made life a little easier for us without having to worry about paying for a house. At a certain point, it became apparent that the living situation was not ideal for anyone. I moved all of my stuff into my grandfather's house. He lived alone at that time, was going through chemotherapy, and my living in that house helped far beyond what I could ever imagine. It also gave my grandfather a little something to look forward to every day. Nate didn't move in with us right away. It took some convincing for him to actually want to leave his mom and be with his fiance and child. We lived with my grandfather for free. All we had to do was pay our own bills. My grandfather helped us in every way possible. He was so good to me and always wanted what was best for me. He saw how hard I worked to give my daughter the best life possible. He also saw how I would be out of the house at 7:00 am to bring my daughter to daycare and then myself to work, while Nate slept until about 10:00 am, threw some clothes on, and went to work for his father. My grandfather took care of me because, in his eyes, Nate wasn't meeting his standards.

I started resenting Nate for not pulling his weight, or rather the weight I expected from him. I was mad that my grandfather, who had cancer, had to help support us. I was mad he slept until 10 am. I pushed those feelings down and kept moving. Addressing those issues would snowball into so many things, and I didn't want to open Pandora's box.

Years went by, and Nate and I wanted two different worlds. He loved living a minimalist life, and I worked more and more because my soul needed more from life. He would stay up all hours of the night and sleep all day. I wanted someone to enjoy life with, and instead he was either tired or working. I couldn't do any of this anymore. I felt myself slipping away. I started going out with my girlfriends and friends from work. I wondered what life would have been like if I had never gone back to Nate and married someone else. I was checking out. The reasons I was staying were not fair to him or my daughter. My daughter deserved to see two parents who loved and respected each other. She deserved to see a partnership. While Nate may have changed his cheating ways when we said I do, respecting me was still an issue. How can you say you respect your wife when you watch her struggle every day to get her and her daughter out of the house while you lie in bed? How can you respect your wife when she took on extra jobs such as tutoring or stipend positions at school to pay the bills and you used your paycheck for season football tickets? I was exhausted, and respecting me in one way doesn't mean I don't deserve respect in another. My mind drifted back to the days when I would buy Nate things for his attention. It may be presenting itself differently, but let's face it, I was taking care of him again, years later. I felt triggered by this every day, and my anxiety had me spiraling. I needed to decide if I was all in and would work harder or if the writing had been on the wall for eight years and I was missing it.

I sent a text message to an old friend explaining how I was feeling. He was the only guy I still kept in touch with somewhat, and as I was contemplating what to do next with my life, I thought opening up to him might help. I needed a guy's point of view. I needed to know that if I left Nate, I wouldn't just be viewed as the divorced mom. He was always honest with me and knew how to get me out of my spiraling thoughts. He was my best friend for a moment in time when I was younger. We spoke briefly through text, making me realize I missed our friendship that had faded over the years. In the end, he told me he couldn't be a part of breaking up a family, but if I ever did decide to move forward with a divorce—by my OWN choice—he would be there for me. After we spoke, I felt the level of confidence I needed to finally move on from Nate. This was not because I intended to be with anyone else. I gained my confidence because this advice was from someone outside of "our circle." My close friends had already formed an opinion of him, so asking for their advice would always be: leave. When I asked my friend his opinion, he told me that what mattered was what made me happy, which in turn would make my daughter happy. That is all I have ever wanted. When Nate got home from work, his face was visibly bothered. He had asked my mom to come over to watch my daughter. He wanted to go for a drive and talk. I had no idea what for, but maybe he sensed my distance. We got in the car, and he slammed on the gas, tires squealing. Let me remind you that driving, in general, was one of my triggers. He knew that. Was he doing this to scare me? What was happening? He started screaming at me so loudly that my nervous system literally shut down. I automatically went into fawn mode. I didn't speak. I didn't move. He drove down the main road in town, his speed accelerating with each second. He told me the text I sent to my friend was forwarded to him. He asked me if I thought the people who I thought were my "friends" wouldn't tell him? He angrily asked if I thought they had more respect for me than him. He told me I was disgusting. He told me my friend thought the same, and that's why he copied him on the text. He told me people respect him more than they respect me, and to remember that.

    I couldn't talk. I was so confused because the conversation I had just had with my friend was in confidence. He told me he didn't want to be the reason a family broke up, so why would he send that text? It didn't make sense. Nate went on and on about how awful I was. I zoned in and out, trying to process it all. Then he said something that stopped me dead in my thoughts.

He told me if I embarrass him like that again, he swore he would drive this truck right off the road. Do I think he was being literal? No. Could he have, been in the state that he was acting? Absolutely. He was already driving irrationally and dangerously, and I had no idea if he would really just drive us off this damn road. "Okay. Okay. I'm so sorry. I will fix this. We can go to therapy, and I promise we can go back to being a happy family." I didn't want any of that. I was scared. I was threatened. I did what I had to do to prevent myself from having a nervous breakdown right then and there. I needed to get home to my daughter. He continued his rant, telling me I was unstable. He told me that I needed to be on medication and that he thought I was bipolar. He wanted me in a psychiatrist's office that week, on top of therapy.

When we got home, I put my toddler to sleep and lay in bed. I replayed the night's events over and over. Why would my friend do this to me? Why would he send Nate the text? I was blindsided by him, and I felt betrayed. I thought he was someone I could talk to, and instead I was being set up in a scenario that involved so many of my triggers. If this is what guys were like, then I was better off just staying here with Nate, where my grandfather kept me safe. It's easier to stay in a broken marriage than it is to have the courage to start over. I took the easy way out for many reasons, but mostly because I don't think I was in a mental space that could handle all the repercussions of a divorce. If someone, who was my good friend at a certain point thought I was disloyal or disgusting for wanting something better for myself, then what would other people think? If Nate was this mad right now, imagine if I said I wanted a divorce. The next day we started couple's therapy, and you guessed it, I was in the psychiatrist's office.

I started the couple's session by explaining why I was in a bad place

from broken to beautifully broken

mentally and emotionally with my husband. I explained how I started to feel those feelings of resentment resurfacing. Even though the things he did to me were prior to marriage, I still couldn't move on from the hurt. We started by talking about the abortion, and the sessions just flowed from there. During couple's counseling, I became pregnant with my son. I was happy. Having my son gave me a distraction from my crumbling marriage. My entire focus was on my daughter and my newborn. As you can guess, the patterns of feeling like I didn't have a partner in life started up again. When my son was born, it was near Valentine's Day. That was a busy day where Nate worked. He didn't stay the whole time at the hospital with me or when I first got home. He went right to work. Coincidentally, when my daughter was born, it was around Mother's Day, another busy time at work. My mom drove me to the hospital, and after she was born, Nate returned to work, coming back and forth to see us. I never came before his job that barely paid our bills. Nate was okay with the lifestyle we had. He was happy with just getting by with the help of my family. We didn't live a bad life. We had an acre of property and an in-ground pool. My grandfather was a blessing to us. The thing is, it wasn't OURS.

As the years passed, I wanted more. I wanted to own my own house. I wanted to take vacations and buy things without having to save up for them. Nate was comfortable. Nate didn't need more. I realized if I wanted more, I would need to make it happen on my own. I started an event planning business on the side in addition to teaching and tutoring. Nate still worked with his dad. I asked if he would consider a job that maybe paid more money or an additional job, and he told me if I wanted more, then I should get another job. We weren't on the same page. We were never on the same page in the 13 years I knew him. It was time.

Divorce is one of the hardest things you will ever go through. It doesn't matter if you are the one who wanted it or if you got served the papers. It is torturous. To say the words "I want a divorce," and know as soon as you let them out, you will ultimately be changing someone's life is hard. Telling your kids their parents are getting divorced is gut-wrenching. I knew that Nate would be happy with someone who appreciated him for who he was eventually, and he would align with someone who shared the same dreams as he did. Unfortunately, to get to that point, hearts would be broken. I knew my children would be better off seeing their parents happy instead of always fighting, but before that time came, I had to rip away the only life they knew, shake it up in a bottle, and hope it would all settle without exploding.

A divorce is dirty. It doesn't play fair, and in the end when you sign those papers, it's like a funeral. I didn't show much emotion through the divorce process because my psychiatrist had me severely medicated. I also felt like I had to be strong to not buckle under all this stress. I asked for the divorce, yes, but that doesn't mean I didn't mourn the loss of so many things. It's like being at a funeral with an empty casket. All the things I had dreamed my life would be were dead. Every vision I had for my future? In the empty casket. My relationship of 13 years? In the casket. Even if I could maintain a cordial relationship with my ex, it would still never be the one I had. That's gone. Before you decide to make such a huge change in your life, you really need to consider what you're putting in that casket and if it's what you really want.

What hurt me the most was being the one who had to disassemble my family unit. I had to watch my ex-husband pack all his bags while my kids cried. I had to console my son late at night when he wanted to lay with his dad. I had to hand over my children on a Friday and not see them again until Monday after school! I had to go DAYS without knowing a thing about my kids. It broke me. On the weekends I didn't have my kids, I hurt badly. I tried to cram a million activities into a weekend to distract myself. Sometimes those activities involved drinking with friends to numb my emotions. Old habits don't die. It did become easier with time, but I still always worried. The entire divorce process is unfair from beginning to end, stressful and ultimately

from broken to beautifully broken

heartbreaking. This won't be easy, but if it's what you truly want, then it will be worth it. Don't waste your time figuring out whose fault it was. It doesn't matter. It doesn't matter how you got here or who hurt who. What matters is that you find peace for YOURSELF. Revenge and retaliation are for the immature. Focus on yourself and how you can be happy again.

What I Know Now

Marriage is a joint venture where both parties want to help the other fulfill their own dreams. They want to stand by each other's side and cry together, laugh together, be scared together and celebrate together. Sure, marriage takes some level of compromise, but before you marry someone, you really need to know what is not compromisable. What are your "hard nos." What do you want for yourself in life that you aren't willing to give up? Find a partner who is happy to share that dream with you and doesn't expect you to relinquish any of that dream. Find a person who has their own goals and is adamant about fulfilling their own dreams. Together you can find a way to both have your happily ever after. Some small steps take compromise, of course, but THE BIG PICTURE is untouchable for both of you.

I wish I had been honest with myself and Nate from the beginning. Raising a child by myself would have been better than her seeing what was later going on in my marriage. What my daughter essentially saw was to settle, let others make decisions for you, and when you make a mistake, you need a punishment. My best advice is before you jump into a marriage ask yourself a few things. So many things that I never even thought of in my early 20s are now crucial in my 40s. Before you say yes to a proposal or propose, there are a few key things I would advise you to consider.

Finances. This is not shallow. This is not being a "gold digger." This is pure mathematical revelation. What is this person's work ethic?

Does this person put work before family? Is this person on the same trajectory as me? Meaning what kind of lifestyle are they comfortable with? There is nothing wrong with any amount of money a person makes, BUT if you want a lifestyle that is different from your partner's, then money becomes a topic to consider. What value does your partner put on the dollar? Do they want to save their money for a rainy day or an emergency fund, or are they a free spirit who wants to enjoy making memories and having experiences with their money? Do they expect you to split the bills of life 50/50, even if you make less or more money than them? AND if so, does that mean the responsibilities of the home and family are split as well? Most of the time, one partner always feels like they are contributing more in some way, and this can turn into resentment. It's important to talk frequently about how you are feeling and be open to switching up the way things are going if one person is feeling taken advantage of. Relationships are not always 50/50. Sometimes it's 80/20, and that's alright. Sometimes you and your partner will need help or a break, and you'll have to pick up the slack. That's fine, so long as it's a reciprocal process. THIS TAKES WORK! Money is so important. Finances can break your marriage before it has a chance to survive.

Second, is **Parenting**. This is crucial. First of all, do they want children? How many children do they want? Do you both want to go to any extreme to have a child, or are you okay with living a life with just the two of you should it not happen naturally? What is the plan for children? Will you both work and have childcare for the baby? Will your partner work while you are a stay-at-home parent, or will you work while they stay at home? As my children got older, I found it very hard to stay on the same page with my partner because our parenting skills or approach were different in so many ways. We still work on this to this day. The key is that we work on it, and we don't give up.

How is this person as a **Caretaker**? Can you picture this person by your side, nurturing you and helping you should you become ill or need surgery? I have seen many marriages where the husband has gone right back to work after their wife was in labor or had surgery, and she was left to recover on her own. Some women love that independence, so this is a non-issue. Some women need to know that their partner will support them and stay by their side for as long as they need them. When my grandmother was diagnosed with cancer, my grandfather was helpless. He was scared and wanted to be a nurturer, but he JUST WASN'T. My aunt took care of her; my dad took her to some doctor appointments; I painted her nails and tried to make her laugh. My grandfather just kept thinking about what his life would be like without her. I love that man, I really do, but he was not a nurturing man.

Family. Your partner's family becomes yours whether you like it or not. Whatever issues your partner has with them, whatever the dynamics are of your partner's family, they are now yours too. If you don't get along with a particular person in their family, is this something you really want for the rest of your life? Are you willing to swallow your pride and mend that relationship for the sake of your love?

Love is an amazing feeling. It's a raw emotion that should be embraced. Love, unfortunately, doesn't make a marriage. This is where people sometimes get confused. Sure, you can love someone, but marriage is WORK. It's one of the relationships you'll have in life that will need constant work. If you're not working on your marriage in some capacity, it will slowly fade, and that road is a slippery road to take. Don't get me wrong, marriage shouldn't be so much work that it leaves you exhausted and feeling defeated. Marriage should be the type of work where you feel like you're bettering yourself each day. Marriage is the type of work that makes you feel proud when you've overcome a hurdle. It's like going to therapy. It's a lot of work, but it's GOOD, HEALTHY work. Marriage is the same. You should be constantly getting to know your partner on different levels, and when you stop putting in the work, when you stop trying, you may find yourself in front of an empty casket.

It Only Took 13 Years

I met my husband the same exact summer that I met my ex-husband. The same month actually. It was freshman orientation at our college, and I was with my best friend Jane. During this two day orientation, we were teamed up with a random stranger, and we slept in the dorm together for the night. Jane and I decided to ask our roommates for the night if they would mind swapping spots so that Jane and I could dorm together. They were totally cool with it. As we went around campus exploring different things, we bumped into a boy we knew from town. We said hello, and he introduced us to his friend, Christian. I thought he was cute and slightly cocky, but I had a boyfriend and was going through an awful breakup process. We invited them to our dorm after the orientation was over for a small "party". Needless to say I barely spoke to him that night and I never saw him again for quite some time. I really thought he might have looked my way just once, but with my self confidence issues I wasn't betting on it. In fact, he ended up spending the night talking to the girl who was supposed to be my roommate.

Months passed, I broke up with my boyfriend and was "talking to" Nate. If one would call it that. One of my other good friends asked me to come out with her to meet her new boyfriend. I really didn't love the idea of being the third wheel, but she managed to convince me somehow. Jackie introduced her new boyfriend to me, and as he turned

from broken to beautifully broken

to say hello, I realized it was Christian. At first, I was slightly uncomfortable knowing that I did think he was good looking and he was dating my good friend, but I had enough drama with Nate, and it would only be weird if I made it that way. Why did he find my friend attractive but not me? Why did he ask her out, but never spoke to me? Here I was questioning my self-worth and looks yet again. We actually ended up hanging out quite often. Jackie would invite me out often since Nate never did, and Christian would invite his friends out, and we would go out as a group. We had fun, and I realized he wasn't as cocky as I thought he was. He was surprisingly really quiet. As Nate and I eventually got serious, Jackie and Christian broke up. I never saw him again for 13 years!

After I separated from my ex-husband, in August of 2013 I moved back into my mother's basement. Me and my two kids put an entire house worth of stuff into a basement and stayed there until I could figure out what to do next. It wasn't so bad. My mom helped a lot with the kids, and when they went to their dad's for the weekend, I didn't have to be alone. One night as I was unpacking my millionth box of stuff, I looked around the room. The room that was once a hangout for me and all my friends now held my entire life. I noticed the walls were the same color as the ceiling and the trim. It was awful. I thought to myself, why would my mom do this? Then I remembered. She didn't do this; Jackie, Christian and I painted this room drunk one night during college. It made me wonder what he was up to all these years later. I messaged him on Facebook, which took every courageous bone in my body. I literally had no idea if he was married or dating or if he even remembered me! I hit send and threw my phone down. I couldn't look.

To my surprise, Christain answered me. After some small talk, he told me I should go to a certain lounge a few days later. I gathered up my girls, got dressed up and went to that lounge. I didn't know if he would be there, but at least I would have a much needed night out with my girls. I was going through my divorce and was approaching the final date when it would all be over. I was stressed, depressed, angry and I just needed a night! We had so much fun. We laughed and danced and acted silly like we were still in high school. Then I spotted Christian across the room. He saw me, I know he did! Get this, he saw me and then turned his head away. He didn't come over and say hello. He stayed where he was and kept talking to everyone else!

I refused to let this bother me. I had been through so much in life, that, at this point, it was whatever. If he wasn't coming by me, then I was over it, for real this time. My friends and I were still having so much fun and wouldn't leave any time soon. We continued laughing and dancing and drinking without skipping a beat. I have THE BEST friends. All of these girls showed up for me. They had husbands, kids, jobs and their own "stuff," but they came out on a Wednesday night FOR ME. That's what you look for in a friend and a partner, someone who knows you need them so badly without even saying it out loud. I love all those girls for exactly who they are.

Shortly later, as I walked to use the bathroom, Christian grabbed my arm. After a brief hello, I continued walking. When I walked out, he was still there. He walked over by me and my friends and bought us all drinks. He stayed with us the whole night and even took me to eat later that night for Jersey's famous cheese fries with gravy. He explained that a friend of my ex-husband had approached him and told him "not to think about going near me." He kept his distance for a little bit that night but then ultimately decided to do what he wanted, which was be with me. The rest is history. We dated from then on. It was a real relationship. It was give and take. He showed me love in ways I didn't think possible. He loved me at one of the lowest points in my life, despite my cracks, my baggage and my history. At a certain point months later, I introduced him to my children. They loved him, and he really cared for them like his own children. We eventually moved out of my mother's and into a one year leased apartment. This would give a trial run for everyone. I needed to make sure my kids were comfortable living with Christian and vice versa before it was permanent. Christian was living his best bachelor life prior to this, so there were lots of big changes happening. I didn't think he could handle all my "baggage" because of my constant lack of confidence, but he did. Not only did he handle it, but he embraced it. He co-parented my four and eight year old. He was everything I never had. We bought a house together and got engaged in a sunflower patch with my kids present. He was what my heart needed my whole life. He gave me confidence, strength, and courage to be my true self. Today we have successful businesses, three children, a beautiful home and a healthy relationship. It was possible to be loved again. It was possible to be loved in the right way. It was possible for someone to love me enough to want the best for me, to protect me. It was possible to settle that inner child who wanted someone to care enough about her, to protect her and spend time with her. Christian was all the things my soul needed to recover. For that, I am forever grateful.

What I Know Now

Take the chance. Do something outside your comfort zone! Despite Christian not paying me any attention the few times we had met previously, I still took a chance and messaged him. I ended up understanding what a real relationship was from that one little courageous act of messaging him. He taught me how I should be treated as a woman, mother, girlfriend and eventually wife. I ended up marrying that man! Can you imagine if I didn't somehow find the strength to type that one little message? My whole life would be different. Maybe I should have taken the first step that night at college orientation. Maybe we weren't meant to be together then. I could sit here and wonder about all my maybe's, but you don't have to! You can take the chance now. If you want something, get it. Don't let anyone, including yourself, tell you you're not worthy of it. I promise you'll surprise yourself. My therapist during my stay at the hospital told me something. She said, "Stop *should*ing on yourself." What she meant, in a kind of comical way, was stop saying I should have or I shouldn't have. Just do it and OWN it, regardless of how it turns out. You stepped towards something you wanted or didn't, but it was your OWN choice!

Christian sounds like your typical soulmate story, right? We crossed paths. The universe kept putting us back together. We were always meant to be. Sure, that may be true, but make no mistake, we work to stay together. When I first started dating Christian, there were definitely some dynamics that had to change, but I am sure he thought the same of me. No one is ever 100 percent perfect for each other. Marriage is work. That's it. There's no way around it. You need to compromise and adjust. You need to empathize and be supportive while not losing yourself and your own visions. You need to swallow your pride and put your ego aside. It's a lot of work. You see, most people ask themselves the wrong question about whether this is "the one." They ask themselves if they fight often, do they put me first, or do they love me? Sure, those are important, but so is this: is this person someone I am willing to fight for every day? Is this person worth the compromises and the rough days? Is this person someone I will stand by through life's obstacles, even if it's not so fun? If your answer is no, then this is not your person. I've never seen a marriage, a successful marriage, where partners always saw eye to eye. There will be differences, but there are so many more good times. There will be times when you'll argue. That's what life is about, right? How boring would conversations be if everyone had the same opinion or view on things? The question is, can this person communicate with me in a way that allows me to express myself without turning it into an argument? There are milestones and celebrations. There are so many little things that make you smile every day. So I guess the questions shouldn't be, do we always agree, does he put me first, does he love me? What it should be, is will I STILL love them on the days they don't do any of those things? Will I still value our marriage on the rough days, and vice versa? Life will always be complicated. What you need to decide is who you'll want by your side when it does, and my answer will always be Christian.

Rainbows, Sunrises and Sunsets

Grief is not at its greatest at the time of your loss. Grief is a bandit that sneaks in and out of your life when you don't expect it, haunting you with heartache. It doesn't matter the age of the person you lost; it doesn't matter how long or how well you knew them; it doesn't matter how you lost that person, grief is grief, and any loss is traumatic. Some of my losses were harder to get over than others, but make no mistake, each time you lose somebody, a piece of you goes with them. I have experienced grief and loss in many different forms, and each time it has affected me differently.

My grandparents and uncle were all very important people to me. I was so close with each of them and managed to somehow spend their final hours with them. I even held both of my grandmother's hands as they took their last breath. My noni passed away from cancer at 69 years young. She was diagnosed in November and was only with us until April. It was the first time I lost someone so close to me. The sadness overtook me. I had no idea how to handle this kind of pain. No matter what I did or how I did it, there was nothing I could do to bring her back. I spent every single day with her in hospice. Watching someone fade away is the most helpless you'll ever feel in your life. You want to scream to make them stay, but some invisible force is holding your mouth closed. You can barely breathe. It's days of constant grief and sadness until they finally pass. Then it's days of sadness when you least expect it for the rest of your life.

My grandfather was a little bit harder on me. I had lived with him through his chemotherapy and surgeries for six years. Every time he got better, he ended up getting sick again shortly after. On the morning I left for Disney with my two kids, my grandfather called 911. My aunt met us at the house and went with him to the ER. As the medics rolled him out, he looked at me and said, "Ella, this is the last time I'll be in this house," a tear falling from his eye. He was always a little dramatic, so I didn't actually think it would be. He wasn't wrong. From the emergency room, my grandfather was admitted to the hospital on the hospice floor, the same floor where we lost my grandmother. It was like Groundhog Day, except this time my heart was barely pumping. I was broken. I couldn't imagine living without him. I couldn't imagine my son not going downstairs to his kitchen in the morning to eat waffles with him.I couldn't imagine not taking care of him, and him not taking care of me.. I couldn't imagine any of it, and I had to take a break. I left hospice for a few hours, and that's when my father called me to let me know he had passed away. I wrote his eulogy and read it in front of the entire church. No matter how much medication I took that day, there was no getting through that eulogy without a breakdown. I gasped for air so loudly that my brother asked if I needed to go outside. I think that loss for me was the hardest. I loved that man like a father, and I always will.

My uncle, who happens to be my godfather, was also diagnosed with cancer. His cancer did not last very long either. I remember going to visit him at his house, which unbeknownst to me, was the night before he passed away. I was explaining to him my situation with my ex-husband, and I was debating on if I should move on or not. He lifted his head from the table, and with all his strength, he told me, "No matter what you decide, I support you, and I am here for you. No questions. I love you." That was the last time I spoke to him. He left behind two beautiful girls and a wife who was deeply in love with him.

They had the kind of love I always admired. My uncle called my aunt his bride even all those years later. He was a good man, and life is a little less bright without him.

My grandmother just recently passed away, and her passing was not any easier than the others. She lived only a few blocks away from me in a senior citizens community. The rest of my family did not live very close to her. Her son, who was my godfather, had passed away. Her daughter, my mother, lived in Florida, and her other daughter didn't drive. In February, my aunt called me frantic. She asked me to go check on my grandma. She had been calling her since last night and that morning there still was no answer. I drove over to her apartment and dialed her number to get buzzed in. No answer. After numerous attempts, the maintenance man, who knew me, let me in. I got up to her apartment and started banging on the door, ringing the bell and shouting her name. She had horrible hearing, so sometimes she couldn't hear the phone ringing or the doorbell even with her hearing aids in. Finally after 10 minutes, the same maintenance man let me in her apartment. He had to cut the chain lock, but I had no other options. To our surprise, the chain lock was off. The lights were all on, and her purse and house keys were on the table. I checked the entire apartment twice, thinking she had fallen somewhere and was passed out, but I couldn't find her. It was a one bed, one bath apartment, so there were not many places she could be. My mind was spiraling, and I went into autopilot. I checked under the bed, in the closet, behind the shower curtain, each time holding my breath for fear of what I would find. She wasn't there. I went up and down the hallways. I knocked on neighbors' doors, I checked the garbage disposal area, I checked the common areas, and I thought my heart was going to implode each time she wasn't in a place I looked.

I told the maintenance man to run the security cameras and see if he could see her leaving the apartment. As he was doing that, I went back to the apartment. There had to be something I was missing. I sat

from broken to beautifully broken

in her chair to regain my composure and take a few deep breaths. That's when I saw it. I saw the sticker backs of the EKG leads on the floor and an alcohol wipe wrapper. The EMTs were here. I called the local police, and I was told she was taken to the hospital last night, but they could not tell me anything more. I fell to the floor and started hyperventilating. Why hadn't anyone contacted us in over 12 hours? If my grandmother was okay, she would have had them call someone. I got a ride to the hospital, not knowing what I was walking into. I headed up to the floor and walked into the room to find my grandmother.

"Hi-ya Hunny! What are you doing here?"

I told her how she gave me a heart attack and possibly a stroke, and then I thought, Oh God, what if that's what happened to her for real? The doctors explained that she had congestive heart failure, and when they arrived at her apartment, she was unconscious. She had dialed 911 and fainted shortly after.

When she was discharged the first week of March, I became her caregiver. My mom flew up, and my aunt came a few times. I hired a company that would come to take care of her a few times a week, and as she needed more assistance as time went by, they would come more often. I would go to check on her almost daily. She broke my heart so many times as she slowly deteriorated. One morning I went there, and she had two table settings for my two older kids. There were waffles with syrup and hot chocolate. When I walked in, she told me the kids were so good for her last night. They played hide and seek, and she couldn't find my son anywhere. She said she made them breakfast, but she couldn't seem to find them anywhere. As my throat developed a lump and I held back my tears, I told her I had to pick them up early and they missed breakfast. I sat with her and ate the ice-cold waffles and freezing hot chocolate. I might throw up later on because only God knows when she made this, but I didn't care. I sat with her, ate with her, and I made her laugh. Although I was so sad to see her mind slipping, it warmed my heart that her mind was wandering back to the times when she would watch my kids for me. This must mean they were important to her, and I couldn't hug her long enough. After that morning, things declined. I had to break the door down once because she fell and was on the floor. She laid there all night long because she couldn't get to the phone. She must have been in the bathroom and fell. She hit her head and then dragged herself to the phone but couldn't reach up to get it. I was dead inside when I saw this. My grandmother, who raised me in my house with my family, was lying on the floor for 10 hours, freezing, with no one to help. I needed a new plan.

I went home and discussed turning our dining room into a bedroom with a hospital bed for my grandmother with my husband. I had a 17 month old baby and two older kids, so it would be a lot, but something had to be done. Until I made a final decision, my mom and aunt were paying for caretakers to spend the nights with her. After only a few nights, I received a call to come over. When I arrived, she was breathing heavily and not waking up. I tried to wake her. I cried, I laid by her, I rubbed her arms… nothing. They told me this was it, and I should say my goodbyes. No. Not yet. I called 911, and the EMTs came. They said they would transport her to the hospital, and she would go through the ER and, if need be, hospice. Again, the damn hospital floor haunted me. I would have lost all three of my grandparents on that floor, and to this day, I will not even go to that hospital if I can avoid it. As the EMTs brought my grandmother down, I grabbed some things, locked up and walked to my car. On my way, the EMT yelled my name. I thought to myself, no God, please don't tell me this is it.

"You wanna take a look into the ambulance for me ma'am?"

Was this guy playing a sick joke on me? Torturing me? He opened the door, and my grandmother smiled and waved, "Hi hunny! I'm okay! My sugar just dropped."

I ran into the ambulance and hugged her. I told her I wasn't leaving her side and that I would meet her at the hospital. " Are you feeling okay? Do you need anything before I get into my car?"

"No. No, nothing at all. We'll be home soon."

I got into my car and waited in the emergency room waiting room for hours! They finally let me in and told me she was being admitted for congestive heart failure and possible pneumonia. I sat by her side and didn't move. She tapped my hand. "Honey, can you find me some pudding?" My grandmother was from Alabama and had the cutest southern accent and the biggest sweet tooth. I found her pudding and fed her every last bite. She giggled about some things the doctors were doing, and she always made me crack up. It was getting late, and I had to get home to the baby for a little bit. I told her that as soon as she got a room, I would be back. I gave her a hug and kiss, waved and smiled as she said, "Bye-bye, see you soon," in her southern charm sort of way. I went home and got the call that she was settled in her room, but visiting hours were over. I could come back in the morning.

At 2:00 am, my son woke up. I had just gotten him back to sleep, walked back into my room and my phone was lit up, ringing. It was on silent, so had my son not been up, I would have never seen this. I answered hesitantly. The doctor on the other end told me that my grandmother coded, but they resuscitated her. She was unconscious, had very labored breathing, and likely was in some pain. I had to decide if I wanted them to keep her comfortable with pain meds, which would likely eventually slow her heart rate down to nothing, or to keep pushing forward with every effort to keep her alive. How could I decide this? She had a DNR, which clearly wasn't followed initially, so I knew the answer she would want. I had power of attorney for the decisions, but this wouldn't be on me. I called my mother and aunt 100 times. No answer. It was 3:00 am so I didn't expect them to answer but a part of me was hoping they would. I called my sister, and she drove in from New York. In the meantime, I got to the hospital first. What I had to see can never be erased. Every detail is finely engraved in my mind. I took off her ring and put it on my finger. I laid my head next to her and waited for my sister and the doctor. The doctor came first. I guess I had to make this decision after all. Her breathing looked absolutely painful. Her chest was rising and falling as if it were about to give out.

"Keep her comfortable. This is no way for anybody to feel."

"I'll go get the kit and be right back."

I talked to my grandmother and told her it was okay to leave us, that we enjoyed every milkshake she made for us, her sweet tea and making us laugh until we peed our pants. Before the doctor even got back to the room, she took her last breath. I was alone. My sister missed her by a matter of minutes. I stood frozen. What happens now?

I wrote a eulogy for my grandmother also, but made my cousin stand nearby because I wasn't sure I could do this, but I did. I emptied out her apartment after she passed and walked out the door one last time. I couldn't believe I would never see her again or hear her say, "Bye bye hunny." It was surreal. Another slow, painful passing my family had to endure. Watching someone get sicker and sicker by the day is hard, but the pain you feel from someone leaving you suddenly, without warning, is indescribable.

My cousin's passing was not like the others and was a complete shock. It rocked our world in a way that words can't explain. My entire family changed on this day, October 1st, 2006. My phone was ringing in the middle of the night over and over again. My daughter was only five months old, so I was exhausted and didn't typically care to answer my phone while she actually let me sleep. This time my phone didn't stop. It was my sister. She was hysterical, and I could barely understand what she was saying. "He's dead. He died."

"Who is dead, Gabriela?"

"I've been calling you, and you didn't answer. He's gone. Matthew is gone. We are all at Zia's house, come here if you want."

I jumped out of bed, told my ex-husband to watch the baby and ran out the front door. No socks on. No shoes on. Barefoot. My aunt only lives two blocks away, and all my body could do was run. When I approached her house, I saw my brother outside pounding on his car. My father was trying to console him. Matt was the same age as him and was his best friend. My brother was supposed to be with him that night. My brother was a mess. I entered my aunt's house, and everyone's heads were on the table sobbing… my sister, my cousins. My aunt was making everyone coffee and tea. No one was thinking about drinking it, but it's what she had to do to keep her mind busy. We were waiting to hear from Matt's parents, my aunt and uncle, but we didn't get the whole story until we visited them the next day. We had never had a loss like this. Matt was in the car by himself driving home from a friend's house. He was in an accident, and we lost him instantly at 17 years old. The grief you feel when you lose someone you love is strong, but when it's a child, you find it hard to wake up in the morning. It's hard to go through your days, it's hard to eat, sleep, talk, function. Your brain can't fully understand this kind of grief. It doesn't make sense how someone young and healthy just said goodbye to you as he headed to a friend's house a few hours prior, and now that goodbye was forever. Watching someone die a slow, painful death is days and days of sadness. Not knowing you are about to lose someone you love so deeply is unfathomable.

In my teenage years and young adult life, I lost very close friends. I lost one to a sudden car accident and another to cancer. Each time it leaves you questioning the universe. It leaves you without faith, fearful and angry. Unfortunately, we have no control over what the day will bring. We don't have a crystal ball to predict the future, and for someone with anxiety, death is our worst fear, consuming our thoughts daily. We are constantly thinking of how to prevent it, what to do, and how to be prepared if we are in a life or death situation. The worst for me is that I lay in bed at night envisioning how I would feel if I lost someone else. I could see the funeral, hear the conversations and read my own mind in my vision. Death consumed my life until I was no longer living. I stopped going to places when the fear became too much. Before I drove somewhere, I would make sure that I had figured out solutions to all possible scenarios that could go wrong enroute. Death was always one of my triggers, but when you lose so many people in such a close period of time, my trigger became a constant state of permanent fight or flight.

The baby I lost before my daughter was a loss. I miscarried a baby before I had my third child, and the cycle happened all over again. I began to fear death before they were even given life in this world outside of me. My miscarriage was difficult. It was my husband's first baby. We heard the baby's heartbeat and were told we were good! A few weeks later, I was bleeding and in an emergency room confirming another loss. My husband was angry. As we know by this point, grief left unresolved is anger. He didn't talk about the baby; he just was sad and mad and needed someone to pay for this. We did genetic testing and found out that the baby had 64 chromosomes and never had a chance. It was no one's fault, except maybe my body's. Maybe the universe was punishing me for having an abortion all those years ago. This was my fault. I pushed those feelings down and decided to put on a happy face and try again. We got pregnant two months after the loss, with TWINS! Maybe God wasn't mad at me. Maybe he sent me two babies because we had lost one. We told our whole family, and they could not believe we were having twins. At our next doctor's appointment, one of the twins had a slower heart rate. We were told to come back in a week. This was the longest week of my life, but after all we had been through, how could we handle anything else? God wouldn't do that to us.

At our next appointment, the ultrasound technician seemed off. She kept avoiding a certain area on my belly, and she wasn't really speaking to us. She would move the machine around and then finally stop at the first twin. She let us hear the heartbeat. We did all the measurements. Then she left the room. I knew what was coming. My eyes frantically searched the huge screen in front of us for any measurements of baby B. Nothing. I only saw information for baby A. The doctor came in to let us know that we had lost our twin. We had one very healthy baby and one angel baby. This is enough loss and grief for a person to handle in itself, but the story continues. I had to go to every ultrasound and see two sacs, one with a growing baby and one getting smaller. I had to carry my baby around, knowing another had passed away right next to him. I couldn't find out the gender of my baby through blood work because baby B was still creating hormones, and so it would be impossible to differentiate which genetics were coming from which baby. At 20 weeks, we found out we were having a boy. Due to the loss of his twin, I had too much amniotic fluid. That, paired with him being breech, led to an emergency C-section six weeks early. We were told to expect the worst but hope for the best. They had all sorts of people in the operating room ready for him. Each person was ready for a different level of crisis intervention, and guess what? He was born perfect. Our rainbow baby and our sunrise baby.

What I Know Now

Loss and grief are a part of life. Some loss is a good thing. It allows the pathways for growth, for the door to open up for new opportunities, even if it's hard to see in that moment. My divorce was a loss, but that broken road led me to my husband. My miscarriages were a loss, but my son would not be here had I let that loss consume me. Without loss, we wouldn't be able to appreciate what we do have. We wouldn't appreciate the small moments that so quickly pass us by. It wasn't until I lost so much I loved that I started to really take in all the moments I had once before taken for granted.

After I lost my noni, I remembered the little things. I remembered how she smelt like sugar (she baked for a bakery). I remembered the way she would smile and the way she would speak really fast in Italian when she was yelling at my grandpa. I remember the way her hands felt when she grabbed my cheeks and kissed me. I remember my grandfather's laugh and his walk and his love for Oggi (the Italian newspaper). It was not the big moments I appreciated. It was all the little things I never noticed until they aren't there anymore.

When my father left, my anger really was unresolved grief and loss. I didn't understand why he would leave all of us. Now when I think of my dad, I think of Blockbuster nights and Parcheesi.—the small things I'll never have again. My grandmother's "Bye bye hunny" and pudding make me smile, for a moment at least. Then I remember how badly I want all of those moments back, and unfortunately, no one can do that for me. All I can do is hold on to those little memories and focus on taking in the present moment.

It's hard in this world today to be 100 percent present. It's hard to put the phone down or keep the email unread. It's hard to skip the laundry or the million errands you have to run, but we have to. We have to find the time, make the time, and be all in. We need to be present with the people we love. It's not enough to just be in the same room or the same house. We need our mind, body and heart to be present. If not, you'll miss those small moments. Having lost so much in such a small period of time, I can say I learned that lesson earlier than most people. I learned life is fragile. I learned nothing is promised, and sometimes, no matter how hard you try, you can't fix something or keep someone from leaving. That's out of our control. What is in our control is having gratitude for our time together. Even though losing people is so hard, I am so thankful that I had the joy and pleasure of getting to know these people when they were here. How lucky am I to have loved someone so much that it makes goodbye this hard. Time can be our greatest gift or our worst enemy. It all depends on what you do with it.

From Mama to Mommy to Mom to Ma

So many things in life change you. Some for the better and some not so much. Becoming a mother has been by far my biggest transformation. It's not something you control. When you become a mother, it's like your brain and emotions and heart all become rewired, and you find yourself suddenly looking in the mirror wondering when you became so grown up and who the heck this new person was who was responsible for the wellbeing of other people!

When I had my daughter, I was young. When I had my first son, I was in my late 20s and when I had my second son, I was approaching 40. Each of these children has changed me in so many ways. They have all made me a better person even if the road hasn't always been easy. I hold my three year old and I find myself wondering when the last time was that I held my other two kids. I rub his back to go to sleep, and I try so hard to remember my very last back rub with my other two, and I can't remember the exact last time. You see, when you're in it, it seems like it will never end. When years have passed, you find yourself asking, how did this all happen so fast? When was the last time my older son said "uppy" or my daughter climbed into my bed? One day it just ends, and you never know when that day will be. They grow up so fast.

With each birth of my children, my anxiety came in like a hurricane. I would look at their little baby faces and wonder how long I had before their faces would change again. Every birthday that passed was bittersweet. It was another year of accomplishments and milestones but also a year older. It was a year further away from when they were a baby and a year closer to them becoming school-aged and then teenagers and then off to college and then…well, you see how this goes. Anxiety kept me wanting to suck up every single moment for fear it would be my last. No one tells you that when you become a mother, worry is your new best friend. I used to lay awake all night and stare at the monitor to make sure my daughter was breathing. Four years later, I did the same with my son, and ten years later when I had my rainbow baby, I was putting my finger under his nose to make sure I felt his breath. I was worried about leaving them with anyone. If I had to leave the house, there was a notebook of directions to care for my babies. Detailed, bulleted, highlighted. I would get so anxious that whoever was watching the kids would skip a part in my notebook that sometimes I would cancel and just stay home! My anxiety was in overdrive.

When my daughter was born, I had postpartum depression that went undiagnosed for a whole year. When my son was born, I immediately knew to seek help after he was born. When my third baby was born, I had postpartum again, then PTSD, then Covid happened. As you can imagine, I didn't leave this child ever. Period. I never returned to work. I never had anyone watch him unless necessary. This went on for at least a year, maybe two. This was the beginning of my relapse into my eating disorder.

Becoming a mother was the most amazing thing that happened to me. It's my greatest accomplishment, but it also changed me to the core. I worried about them constantly. Each year the things I worried about changed, but there was always something to worry about. Your life becomes someone else's, especially in the newborn and toddler years. You eat last, you shower last, you pee when you have a free moment. When they get older, you become the Uber driver. Sports, play dates, after school activities, they all supersede where you want to go. Your life becomes theirs. Everything I needed was on the back burner, I was in constant survival mode just trying to get through my day, and that's fine because, as a mother, I would carry all the weight for them, so they never had to.

It's so true that time is a thief, and I never knew how badly until I had children. I know that each year my kids will be different, and I find myself missing the old versions of them while loving who they are and waiting with anticipation to see what version they will become. Each time I say goodbye to a different version of my children with sadness but also an anticipation to know the new version. Childhood is constant hellos and goodbyes at each and every stage. My brain wants time to slow down, but I also want to rewind and fast forward. It's a roller coaster of emotions that leaves you with a hundred different feelings, but nothing prepares you for the day your baby says mama for the first time. Well, let me rephrase that. Nothing prepares you for that day, BUT ALSO the day they stop calling you mama and say mommy. Then you blink your eyes, and your mom. Another hop, skip, and jump and you are being called from another room by your teenager who now just calls you ma! The first time your baby says mama will melt your heart, but all the others from then on break your heart just a little bit.

When I was 23 raising my daughter, I never wanted help. I wanted to prove to the world that I could do this, and I could do it better than they ever thought. I wore myself out big time. I was battling depression and being all hands on all the time, and I was burning out. When I finally got a grasp on parenting, my son was born. I had serious guilt about not being able to spend as much time with my daughter. I took care of my newborn baby boy, but I also made sure I made time for my daughter as well. I had help controlling my depression this time, but two kids and work had me burning out again. My third baby was born with a whirlwind of emotion. He was a month early. He was breech. I had too much amniotic fluid, and I had lost his twin. So many things could go wrong that it took so much to focus on enjoying my last pregnancy. (Side note: No one ever warns you that you actually miss being pregnant, which makes you kinda sad. You had this baby growing inside you. This baby that went with you everywhere for months, and then all of a sudden they are in the real world, not in their safe little sac, and you miss them, even as you're holding them in your arms).

My last baby was born with an emergency C-section, and we had no idea if he would need the NICU or the level of assistance he would need to breathe. I was a nervous wreck. When he was born, he was perfect. He didn't need any oxygen at all! He didn't need the NICU despite being early, and I finally felt the weight lift off my chest. I was so happy until the doctors had to make sure they got the remains of his twin before they stitched me up. I had lost his twin super early in the pregnancy, but I still had two placenta, two sacs and two babies. When my son was born, I still had to deliver two placentas and whatever remains there were. It was shattering. I was so happy to have a healthy son that I didn't allow myself to process this. I focused my attention on what was happening with him instead of what the doctors were saying, and I pushed those emotions down deep.

Parenting is so rewarding. It's been my hardest job but also my proudest. It's sometimes a thankless job, but I would never change it. My daughter has been with me through all the phases of my adult life. She was by my side before I had my shit together to my proudest moments and every step in between. I apologize to her for bringing her into the world without a plan, without stability, but I would do it over and over again if I had to. My life would not be what it is if it weren't for her. She pulled me out of an unhealthy lifestyle and made me a mother. She is smart and loving and, unfortunately, she had to grow up too early. When I separated from her dad, her and her brother would go every other weekend to his house. Oftentimes she had to take on the role of a parent, and that wasn't fair to her. I can't take back

from broken to beautifully broken

those years for her, but I can be here for her as her friend and protector. I can listen to her when she wants to talk, and I will spend my whole life making sure her and her brothers have the best life they can have.

My middle son was the first boy I had unconditional love for. He reminds me so much of myself when I was younger. I am very protective of him because he is sensitive and kind. He would give you his last dollar. I think he was affected the most by the divorce, which is hard for me to let go of. I tend to favor him even if he's in the wrong because a small piece of me still feels like I traumatized him with the divorce. Don't get me wrong, he loves Christian, and Christian treats him as his own son. He still sees his dad, but I'm talking about the actual moment of his dad leaving. He had to start a new life at an age when he couldn't really understand. He couldn't see how the future would be better for him. He only saw the sadness or the chaos when he was at his dad's as a little boy. I know my son is a handful at the moment as a teenager, getting in trouble, grades falling, but oftentimes, the ones who stay true to themselves, have a loud voice and don't back down and argue their point with you until they are blue in the face, are the ones who become leaders. What drives me crazy now will drive him to be successful later. Not everyone needs to have a perfect GPA to be successful. Character, personality, morals, kindness… these are all more important to me than a letter on a paper, and I am saying that while being a former teacher myself. I know he will do great things in life, despite being born into a broken family. I can't wait to see where his ambition takes him.

My little guy is my miracle. He was not something I ever imagined having until these last few years. I thought my first son would be my last. Then I met Christian and knew, at some point, we would have more sticky fingers and butterfly kisses coming our way. It wasn't easy having my third baby. There were lots of heartaches, disappointment, fear and grief. When we finally could hold this little guy in our arms, I knew the universe gave me a second chance. I was able to relive those baby years with a partner. I was able to have all those small moments together WITH my husband. Somehow the universe knew my little guy would fill a void I never knew I had. I had the chance to do it all over again. I didn't miss one moment of any of my children's lives, but with my older two, I often celebrated and soaked in the small things internally. With my third, it was nice to have someone to experience them with, that I loved and who loved me.

My second son acts ten times his age due to being around his older siblings. He is advanced far beyond his years in maturity, and he gives me a run for my money. Chasing after my daughter at 23 was much easier than chasing after my son at 40.

By the end of the day, I'm exhausted. Sometimes, I feel like I'm dropping the ball with one of my kids. Sometimes I feel like I literally can not do this. I feel three kids at three different major points in their lives is hard to juggle both mentally and physically. One child always keeps me from being 100 percent present with the other. I struggle with giving them their independence and knowing when to intervene.

I think what is so important as a parent is to sit down and really think about what kind of mentor you want to be for your kids. There are many different parenting styles, all equally justifiable. You need to find how parenting makes you comfortable and stick to that. How will you raise your children? What are the most important lessons you need them to learn? What characteristics do you want to see shine?

I think it's also important that, no matter what age, you always get one on one time—a time to check in with your kids. Make it a time that's always a safe space, without judgment or fear of punishment. We all need "our people," and if I'm lucky enough to be a part of my children's "people," then I have attained true happiness as a parent because everything I've done has been for them.

What I Know Now

Being a parent is so hard. Sometimes it can be thankless. Sometimes you feel like you got it all wrong. Sometimes no one even notices how much it takes to actually BE a parent. You'll make the wrong decisions a hundred times while those kids grow up. Some days you'll feel like the superhero, until one little thing goes wrong and you feel like a failure. Mothers are judged no matter what. You need to accept that and grow thick skin. You need to be confident enough in your choices and humble enough to ask others for help or advice. If you choose not to be a mother, you're judged. If you can't have kids, people speculate why. If you have kids early, it must have been a mistake. If you choose to be a single parent, people will assume the other parent left. People will judge you for formula feeding, or getting a nanny, going back to work or not going back to work. The list is endless.

I know that as parents, we often say, my kids come first. While that may have some truth, one must really learn to always put themselves first. That's not to say be selfish, but how can you save the sinking boat if you don't have your life vest on? You can't help them to grow to be the best versions of themselves if you are not the best version of yourself.

Remember, there are so many moving parts to being a parent. What is the sense of having good grades and a good GPA, certificates of achievement, presidential awards and high honor rolls if your child isn't comfortable showing or (even more so) regulating their emotions? What's the point in pushing them to do so well in school if they're not comfortable opening up to you and expressing their true feelings? There's so many ways that you need to teach your child to grow: their mind, their soul, their body. It's important for them to build connections with other people. They need to build healthy relationships with others and themselves. It's important for you to lay the foundation so that these children can be the best version of themselves on their own. It's important for you as a parent to build their confidence and teach them self-love at a young age. It's important as their parents to give them independence while still guiding them. Nobody ever puts enough emphasis on this. We are stuck in this old school mentality where children must obey their parents and respect their elders. They must get good grades and be polite. But how about we teach our kids to use their voices? If they don't agree with what I'm doing as a parent, let's talk about it. Use your voice. Don't silence it for fear of punishment. It's the loudest voices that make the biggest movements. Respect. I do believe children need to respect their parents, BUT parents must respect their children as well. At the end of the day, we're all just humans and we all deserve respect. Once that child becomes an adult, they can choose whether they feel like the level of respect you give them is enough. And if it's not, a child can absolutely build a boundary with a parent. Children don't owe their parents simply because they "parented" them. Respect is earned. It's a two way street, and no child has to put up with a lack of respect simply because you demand something you aren't giving back.

Getting good grades is important. Showing up and trying your hardest is what I expect of my children. Not everyone will have straight As. Everyone learns differently, and everyone has different talents and abilities. Instead of forcing your kid to stay home and read, maybe listen to them a little closer. You might come to learn what their real talent is and what they are passionate about. Those are the things that will make them feel whole. Those are the things that will fill their hearts with pride and, in turn, have self-love.

Being polite and kind is always something a person should carry, but hear me out. Sometimes, being kind or polite makes you feel less if it's not reciprocated. Sometimes being polite allows others to overstep boundaries. So while being polite is important, it's also important to find a way to be kind but also stand firm for your boundaries, and at no point should you ever compromise your confidence or self-worth to be polite. You can be polite to people who deserve it, and that kind of politeness doesn't need to be taught. It's natural human instinct to be kind and polite to those worthy of it.

Being a parent is a lot of emotions, but looking back, I know I must have gotten something right. My kids are good people. They are kind, they have a voice and they are smart and courageous. If, at the end of my life, my children have become good people who make a difference in this world, that will be worth it all. The grades they have, the mistakes they made, the messes I cleaned and the sleepless nights all will be irrelevant. What will matter most is that I leave my children to be better than I was. I raised my children to show love and kindness while standing firm to their beliefs. Help the underdog. It's nice to be a leader, but they should lead while walking beside their peers, not in front of them. Never face your back to someone, and always look a person in the eye. Keep your word and keep an open heart. I may not have done everything right, but my kids are proof that I did something right.

COVID....
A chapter on true mental health

The time that
   Control
   Overtook rationalization & how the
   Venomous bite of
   Isolation
   Destroyed me

I am very specific in this chapter. I want to state only the facts of my experience and what happened to me and my family. This chapter is not about politics or conspiracy theories. It's just about what I went through.

My son was born early in November 2019. In December 2019, my son had RSV, which if you are unfamiliar with, is a very bad respiratory virus that can lead to death in newborns. As a mother of a five week old, I had postpartum, anxiety and sleep deprivation. Now that he was sick with the exact virus I had tried so hard to avoid, my anxiety was at an unthinkable level. I hadn't gone back on my antidepressants since he was born, and that feeling of fear and dread came rolling in like a freight train. I spent Christmas in the hospital with him and away from my other two children. He got better after a few days, and we were told to go home because they had a lot of patients in the PICU with viral infections, and it was safer for him to recover at home from this point forward. When they told me this, they came in with full hazmat suits. I was petrified, and we left immediately. Recovering at home was nerve-wracking, but by the end of January, he was finally better.

March 2020, the whole world went on lockdown. We'd just taken our masks off from the whole RSV incident, and now we had to mask up IF we even left the house. The first few weeks of Covid lockdown were not so bad. We all thought it was temporary, so, when all five of us piled into a house together without ever leaving, we thought there was an end in sight. When weeks turned to months and school never reopened, I started to notice things that part of the world was missing. Every single channel spoke of nothing but depressing, gloomy news. Deaths and piles of bodies, a number on the bottom of the screen tallying up the death totals. Directions of what to do or not to do to stay alive. It was nothing but pure anxiety, worry and uncertainty. Directives were changing daily, and what we did right one day was wrong the next. The world has never locked down before in all the years I was alive, so honestly, I don't believe anyone knew the best way to handle this. What I can tell you is everyone's mental health was certainly not as important as it should have been. It is possible that when making decisions that could affect the entire world, everyone's physical health took precedence. It is possible that our leaders knew our mental health would decline drastically but that our need to stay "Covid free" was of more importance. It is possible that mental health wasn't considered at all. We will never know, but what I KNOW is that the aftermath of lockdown will trickle for years, and for that, I am so fearful.

When my daughter's birthday rolled around in May, we had only been in lockdown for a few weeks. I called all of our friends and family and even our local police station. They led a caravan of cars playing music and honking horns as we stood behind our fence, on our front lawn, waving to those who passed. They placed presents, posters and cards on a small table in front of the fence I had set up. We baked cupcakes and left them out on the table for everyone to take with them. A drive-by birthday. While this makes for a great story, it doesn't take away from the fact that this was a year taken from her.

It wasn't just the small birthdays that children missed, or their moving up ceremony and graduations, it was the big things too. My youngest son spent his first Christmas in the hospital with RSV and his second with just the five of us and a Zoom call of family members. He spent his third Christmas in quarantine because one of my children had Covid. All of his memories of holidays are associated with alienation and isolation. My children opened each of their presents in front of the family member who gave it to them on a Zoom call or Facetime. We talked to family members through windows. We would set up chairs next to the window and outside of the window and talk through the wall. I know some people are reading this and thinking, big deal, at least they are alive and healthy. At least they didn't witness a family member on a ventilator. I am in no way saying that this is worse. I am saying that while my children are healthy physically, it doesn't mean they are healthy mentally. Mental health IS health. So while I am so blessed to have all five of us survive lockdown with only a few episodes of bad Covid symptoms, I am not so lucky when it comes to the emotional toll lockdown took on each and every person in my house.

My older son got Covid and had a runny nose. You know what was worse than that? The emotional breakdown he had from not being able to see his father during Covid. His father works in a place that was considered a highly transmissible area. To be safe, we kept my two older children home with me while their father visited from afar. My ex-husband began a relationship at this time, and my son missed the beginning stages of that. He missed getting to know his dad's new girlfriend and her kids, and when he did finally meet them, they had

from broken to beautifully broken

already formed a close relationship with his father. My son could not control his emotions. He was mad, upset, sad and felt forgotten all at the same time. His father did not choose not to see his son and daughter; the world made that choice for us. In return, my son had an emotional breakdown. The runny nose during Covid was nothing compared to this. Once school started back up, his grades declined, he got in fist fights and received detentions. He was in a bad place mentally. We started him in emergency therapy that was through the state when he made concerning comments about his life. Therapy started immediately but only for a few weeks. From there, we had to find a therapist available for children (most were booked… shocker) and took our insurance. When we found someone, my son started to be able to communicate better using words instead of emotions. It was hard to watch as his mother, especially because no one in positions of power in America thought this was just as important as avoiding Covid. Having an 11 year old boy speak of suicidal thoughts is just as risky as needing a ventilator.

As Covid began to get worse, testing became more readily available. Free tests everywhere. You know what wasn't free? Mental health care. My son's therapist was not free. My son's medications, which we declined, were not free. The assessment to understand his mental health status was not free, but Covid tests were free everywhere. Why was one more important than the other? Covid had physical and mental effects on people, but our nation only focused on the physical.

Both of my two older children have been affected mentally by Covid. My daughter hid her emotions a little bit better than my son, but she was depressed and anxious. She suffered her first panic attack, crying and vomiting, during Covid. She was a straight-A student her whole life. When online schooling started, it was a little bit easier than actual school. When it continued the following school year, it became harder. She didn't understand the material taught through Zoom. For the first time in her life, she was not a straight-A student. To this day, her grades, along with my son's, are a lot lower than they normally were due to the learning gap that was created. Sure, we know about this gap now. Sure, we are trying to fix it in the educational community, but seriously, no one thought of the impact on students and teachers with online learning? The gap is so huge that this generation is struggling to "catch up," and the teachers are overwhelmed, saddened and frustrated that it falls on them.

I was a teacher before Covid. I had left on maternity leave a few months prior to Covid. Once my maternity leave was up, I resigned. I gave up my entire career. 13 years as a teacher and Covid ultimately made me decide to resign. What was asked of teachers was far more than what the pay scale offered, let's keep it real. On top of that, if I had to teach through Zoom, I needed a sitter for the baby, and who is coming to my house during a lockdown to babysit? I resigned and had to deal with my own mental health after that life-changing decision as well.

My nephew was born one month after Covid. His father was unable to attend the birth of his child up until 24 hours prior. They had changed the hospital's rule that fathers could be present literally the day before my nephew was born. No one was able to meet him. No one was able to help my nephew's parents during the newborn stages. No one was able to offer the new mom a break to rest. I met my nephew through the glass window of a car. The first time I was able to actually see my nephew was when he was four months old, outside and I didn't hold him, only his parents did. It was the same with my youngest son. He was only a few months older than my nephew, and no one was able to see him since he was five weeks old. First it was RSV and then straight into Covid. By the time he was able to interact with people, he was extremely introverted. He didn't like being away from me. He didn't know how to act with other people. He'd just started preschool recently, and it was the first time he had been in a room with that many children. It took him a few weeks to understand what being social meant.

Covid not only affected the mental health of children, but adults were getting hit left and right. My husband has never suffered from any form of mental health issues in his entire life. He was extremely lucky in that sense. When our son got RSV, my husband developed PTSD. What might have taken a few months to bounce back from, took YEARS. After RSV, Covid happened, and his PTSD spiraled into full-blown anxiety. He went into fight mode, and he literally locked us down. He was scared of every sniffle, sneeze and cough. He was scared that at any moment, the baby could end up back in the PICU. He was scared that his wife, myself, could die. I have a compromised immune system, so I was considered high risk. He was scared that my son would stop breathing at any moment due to his asthma if he got sick. This fear was not tamed by logic, the news fueled it, the daily mayor reports, the constant internet and social media posts, other people's opinions and, of course, the ever-changing advice of Dr. Fauci. His fears exploded when we were told to do one thing one day and another thing another day. What do you think his solution to all this was? His solution, which ultimately broke me, was to keep us all inside, in his safe bubble, where none of this could happen.

As a person with experience in anxiety, PTSD and depression, I understood his logic. I understood that no matter what I said, his logic would always be the right answer in his mind. His nervous system was stuck in fight or flight mode. So, that's what we did. We bunkered down for a very very long time. Even when the world slowly opened up again, we, as a family, were still cautious. We didn't go places. We didn't have family over unless they tested. The children had to shower immediately after school. We had to wear our masks everywhere. It helped my husband navigate through his mental health. However, it threw the rest of us into our own mental breakdowns. The kids were depressed that they couldn't do normal things. I was depressed and couldn't do ANYTHING. I had quit my job, the lease had been up on my car, and there was no sense in having two cars if we were almost always home. So when my husband left to do something, I was stuck in the house with a toddler and no car, no motivation, no purpose. I understand raising my son has a purpose. However, all of these small changes so quickly made me lose sight of a lot of things. I didn't feel like myself. I stopped getting dressed and stayed in pajamas all day. I stopped accepting invites from my friends to do things because it wasn't worth the argument with my husband. It wasn't worth the effort to get him to see I needed to escape because he could never see my logic or reasoning in his state of mind.

He did not mean for this to happen. He was not punishing us, or trying to keep us to himself. He didn't even like how he acted, but that's the issue. When it comes to brain health, the person suffering can't just "change." Their nervous system is completely out of whack. Their logic is compromised, and their responses to situations are untypical. You know how I know that brain health is not just a genetic issue or something you bring on yourself? I know because my husband has never had any brain health complications in his entire life. This was his first encounter, and it was literally influenced by the world, by society and by leaders he was supposed to trust, instilling a fear so deep that it broke him. His way of dealing with his mental health added fuel to my already spiraling eating disorder.

So many people think that my husband keeping me home during Covid is what "gave me" an eating disorder. My lack of control in life caused me to need to control my food intake and how I looked. That is partially correct. I did need to control something because the whole damn world was out of control. I couldn't protect my kids mentally, and I couldn't give them the life they deserved because real life was stripped from us in so many ways. I couldn't give my kids back the moments they lost forever. That is what fueled my eating disorder. I suffered from relapses for over 20 years, but this time was the worst.

My son was born right before Covid, and as I was physically recovering from his birth, I encountered many issues. My first issue was a hip labral tear. After going for X-rays on my hip to fix the tear, we discovered I had hip dysplasia. I needed a complete hip replacement and femur rotation. I had this procedure during Covid. No one was allowed at my doctor's appointments or to stay for the surgery. No one was allowed to stay in the hospital with me. My husband was allowed to visit for brief periods, but it had to be the same person who always came to visit. I was there for five nights. I had a reaction to the anesthesia, was moments away from a blood transfusion and no one in my family even knew unless they called the nurse's station to check in on me. When I returned home, I had to do physical therapy during Covid.

Shortly after my hip surgery, I ended up needing brain surgery. Again, during my pregnancy, I developed an outpouching on a vessel that extended from my brain to my heart. I needed to fix that and have a bone graft. This surgeon was in a different state than where I resided. I had to drive five hours to this hospital, stay in a hotel alone the night before and check myself in for brain surgery alone. Those two surgeries within themselves are traumas on the body that the body needs to process. Add the fact that the guidelines in both states did not allow for someone to be there with me, and isolation takes on a whole new meaning. While our leaders were trying to protect us from getting the COVID-19 virus, everything that was in place for that affected our brain health.

My grandmother became sick during isolation. She was diagnosed with congestive heart failure and slowly started to forget things. She would talk to herself often and have these delusions that she would swear were real life. I truly believe that when a person is left in isolation for long enough, they will start making scenarios in their head where they interact with other people. The human body and the human brain are not meant to live a life alone. As a society, we are social beings that need interaction, and without that interaction, it forces our brain to create or manifest one. She ultimately died of congestive heart failure, which was not caused by Covid. However, I truly believe isolation led to the onset of that illness. If not the onset, it certainly aided in the quick progression of it. Covid stole my grandmother from me in so many ways I wasn't able to visit her as often as I would have liked during what, unbeknownst to me at the time, turned out to be the last years of her life.

The last birthday song we sang to her was through a glass door. The last holiday I spent with her was with only eight of us. The only place my grandmother went since March 2020 was the hospital. She didn't know the world outside of her little apartment. When I realized her time with us was ending, I needed an outlet. I needed somewhere I could go to help me release my emotions, but guess what? The places one would normally go to during a crisis were forced to be shut down. Churches were closed, so I could not go to pray for her or my family in a place I normally would. Gyms were closed, so I had nowhere to go to let out my frustrations and clear my head. The only place left to go for anyone who needed an outlet was the bars. We could pick up alcoholic beverages and get them in to-go cups, and that is precisely what much of the world turned to.

Without somewhere to practice your faith or somewhere to stay physically healthy, you are forced to exit the reality of this virus through an unhealthy vice: alcohol. I can't speak for the world, but I can speak about the people I know and the stories I have seen or been told. AT LEAST 75 percent of the people I knew were drinking more heavily during Covid. At least half of my friends or family were no longer working out to stay healthy. If you want to know why so many people have fallen into some form of mental illness after lockdown, there are your answers. People were isolated. People lost faith. People became unhealthy, not due to Covid, but due to lack of access to the tools they needed. People used what was available to numb the pain. People were forced to face major problems alone. My husband couldn't be with me for either one of my major surgeries. He also couldn't be there for me when I was broken emotionally and suffering physically.

During the first year of Covid, I found out I was pregnant again. At first, we were completely shocked and in denial. Unfortunately, that shock or denial didn't have too long to settle into happiness and joy because I miscarried again shortly after. I couldn't drive myself to the ER because I was in pain and in no shape to drive. My husband couldn't take me because we couldn't have anyone come to watch the kids, so I called my sister. We wore masks in the car, and she dropped me off. She wasn't even allowed to sit with me in the waiting room. As I entered the hospital, I began bleeding everywhere. I had no one to turn to for help. The nurses told me I could use the bathroom, but at this point, it was uncontrollable. Finally, I was placed on a stretcher in the hallway. The emergency room was so full of Covid cases that there was no room for me. I continued to bleed on that stretcher and eventually started losing consciousness. I came in and out of awareness. It was like I was dreaming and then snapped back into reality for what felt like hours. Once I got examined, they confirmed what I already knew. This time, my husband and I did not cry together while the doctor gave us a minute. This time, I cried alone. This time I had to get myself dressed and call my sister to get me. This time I had to process all of that alone. My husband had to wait at home to hear what was happening. When I let him know, he had to sit with that news alone, but also maintain composure to watch the three kids.

What was happening in the world was unfair. Covid taking lives was unfair. Covid stealing moments from us was unfair. What do I think was the most unfair? What was most unfair was the disregard for society's mental health. Whether it was an oversight or pure ignorance, or done exactly as I said, it doesn't matter! People committed suicide due to loneliness, and my son expressed some of those exact feelings at such a young age. People lost time, memories and special moments. All of those things will take years to recover from, long after the virus severity is gone. When is our nation going to acknowledge that mental health IS health? When are they going to make decisions based on all aspects of health? Until that happens, we must fight for more awareness.

What I Know Now

Hindsight is 20/20, right? So maybe some of my thinking here is because I know for a fact that a lot of the things I did for my family were wrong. A lot of the things my husband did for our family were wrong. I also know that what our leaders did to this country was wrong. Mental health was not at the forefront of their minds when making worldwide choices. The effects of isolation, lockdown, separation and loss were not proactively thought of. Today, our leaders are being reactive in the sense that they are providing some outlets for people who struggle with their mental health. My son's school has a free psychologist that visits once a week for sessions with certain kids. He is one of them. Telemed therapy was being offered at a reasonable rate. The problem here is that it was done REACTIVELY. I fear for the young children who missed out on socialization, school, sports, activities—NORMALCY. I fear for the elders who had to be away from the world as their health deteriorated and their minds began slipping due to lack of human interaction. I fear for the teenagers who missed out on their major milestones. You can't get those moments back. Those moments were ripped away from these kids and can never be recovered. That is mentally traumatizing. They had to accept, essentially, a loss. The loss of prom, graduations, trips, sweet 16s, the list goes on.

We have a big problem that needs to be fixed, and as we all know, damage to your brain's health can take years to recover from. I don't think I will ever get over my anger for missing moments with my grandmother. I won't easily get over the trauma of being alone for major surgeries and losing a baby. In fact, it was proven to be true when I developed my eating disorder. All these things affected me so much that I was close to organ failure. It is so important to look at mental health and your brain's health as A PART OF your health. It's time to open our eyes and realize that life can break you down and that getting help is okay. You don't have to bottle all of it up inside and wait to explode. In my opinion, I would have changed it all. I would've masked up and spent hours with my grandmother instead of fearing I might get her sick. I would have allowed my children to see more family, and not just through a window or six feet away. I would have accepted the invitations to go to friends' houses instead of fearing the virus. I understand that my choices may be very different from yours. Covid may have affected you in devastating ways, so isolating was the right choice for you, but it wasn't for me. It will take a long time to fix the long-term effects of Covid on my family, and for that, I am somewhat at fault.

A child feeds off the vibes sent out by the adults in that household. If I wanted my kids to be fearless and strong, they were in the wrong damn house. What my husband and I exhibited fueled the way they reacted to Covid. Part of my eating disorder recovery is owning that and accepting that I can't fix the past, but I can change the future. I can ensure my family and I have the right tools to speak with someone when needed. I can make sure that my children engage in social activities. I can make sure that I make up for lost time with the family I still have here. I can make sure my husband knows he can talk to me when he feels like the world is starting to cave in. I can bring joy to my home when the world is filled with uncertainty, sorrow and anger. I can give my kids the space to speak freely without judgment. Covid did a lot of things, but one thing I won't allow it to do to my family is break us anymore. We are healing slowly but surely. It will take time, patience and grace, but I intend to do everything possible to get my family the support they need to thrive in a world that shut down on us.

So what's my silver lining? I will never take advantage of the things I can do freely. I will never take for granted the ability to hold or hug or kiss someone without fear. I will never allow another person to hold my freedom in their hands. Doing so made me very sick. As a mother, we often put ourselves last, and that truth carries over into a marriage sometimes as well. All I thought about was how to help my husband and kids, but I forgot to help myself. I will always take back the control that is rightfully mine. Also, I stay away from the news as much as possible. I find that it rarely highlights a happy story. Most of the time, it fills us with fear, sorrow or anxiety. Instead, I choose to look around me and find the good things that happened in the world, my state, my town or even my home.

I won't lie, in the beginning of it all, having my husband and kids near me all day every day was selfishly comforting. I had a newborn, and when they were home I was a little less lonely. What kept me from being lonely at first ended up keeping my family lonely from the rest of the world. Make no mistake, even though isolation truly took its toll on us, we, as a family, took our power back. We control the fate of our lives. We control what we do and don't do, and no one will dictate otherwise, especially if it will affect our mental health.

Sticks And Stones May Break My Bones...But My Eating Disorder Almost Killed Me

On March 30th I used every ounce of strength my body had and went to the emergency room escorted by my sister in law. It was not by choice. I was forced by family members who had gotten together and created an intervention. When I arrived at triage, the woman behind the desk asked me why I was there. My response: "no idea." My sister in law explained to the woman that they believed I was malnourished and suffered from an eating disorder. They wanted me to have a psychiatric evaluation and to be medically assessed. I sat in the waiting room, unable to process what was happening. All I could do was wrap my sweater around me to try and stop my body from shivering. I was cold. I was tired. I wanted to go home. This was ridiculous.

After what felt like 42 hours, I was brought into a room in the ER. The nurses told me I needed an IV and bloodwork, and the doctor would be in shortly. My blood pressure was below normal. My heart rate was below normal. I was dehydrated. My fingers, especially the tips, were purple. My bloodwork came back with almost no white blood cells and a whole plethora of things out of whack. My EKG came back with some abnormality. The doctor came and told me they didn't have a psychiatric unit at that particular hospital, but he would give me some nutrients through the IV. I looked at my sister in law, who had been patiently sitting with me for six hours, and told her: "I told you so. Totally a waste of time. I'm fine." She stopped the doctor because if you knew my sister in law, you would know this was not acceptable for her. She knew something was wrong, and she wasn't leaving until we had a plan. She asked the doctor at what point he thought I would need to go into treatment for an eating disorder and what signs she should look for. His immediate response was, "Now. She should be there now. I just don't have the capacity to help in the way she needs it." With that, I finished my IV and headed back home. I went to my primary care physician the next day. In the meantime, my entire family was calling various eating disorder treatment centers to see what would fit me. Many were only for adolescents; many were far. My husband managed to get me an appointment for an assessment at a hospital about an hour away in a few days. While at my primary care physician, I prayed she would say it was all a misunderstanding and everyone could just relax. Instead, I got quite the opposite. She spoke to me as if I were broken. Her soft voice started explaining to me, in almost a childlike fashion, that my blood work all pointed to malnutrition, and if I continued at this rate, I would begin organ failure. She wrote down a few recommendations that were all inpatient. I stood up off the patient chair, and everything started going black. I laid back down, my face tinted a gray color. All I kept thinking was, *how is this happening?* and *how the hell am I at this point in my life?* This didn't make any sense. I was fine.

Over the next few days, I arranged for someone to watch my three children. I packed a bag in case I had to stay. I was told no pens, no shoe strings, no cell phones, no hoodies or drawstring pants. I wasn't allowed to have a razor or any sharp objects. There was no way I belonged there, but I packed to appease my family. Tuesday came, and my kids cried as I got into the car. I couldn't even tell them when I

from broken to beautifully broken

would see them again. I was just as lost as they were, and it was infuriating. The last few days had been nothing short of traumatic for them and my husband. They didn't know where I was going, for how long, how sick I actually was or wasn't, and how their own lives would look during all of this. My husband drove me to my intake assessment appointment. Here they would perform blood work, EKG, urine analysis and, of course, weigh me. I wore my heaviest terry cloth pants and sweater. The scale was no stranger to me! I was weighing myself every time I walked into the bathroom. When I brushed my teeth, when I used the bathroom, when I showered, after I ate, before I ate and even some random times in between, I always stepped on that scale. This scale was different, and it pissed me off. It was covered with cardboard so I couldn't see the number. Are you serious!? Moments later, the psychiatrist pulled me into her office for an interview. It's a bit of a blur, but I remember her being stern and to the point. "Walk me through your day Ella."

"I have a two year old, so my day is never the same. I don't work. I'm a stay at home mom and housewife, but I used to be a teacher for 13 years before Covid."

"What does your breakfast consist of?"

"Coffee."

"Coffee and?"

"Coffee with milk and sugar."

The psychiatrist scribbled something down and then asked when I ate my first meal. I told her it varied but mostly around 2:00/3:00. I mean, when I was in college I woke up at this time. It's not awful to eat for the first time at 2:00.

"What does that meal look like?"

Here we go. "A breakfast bar. And I'll just make this easier for you. I don't eat again until dinner. I do eat whatever I cook for my family, but under certain conditions."

"Which are?"

"I allow myself to eat dinner if I didn't eat anything besides the breakfast bar. If I eat something else during the day, I don't eat dinner."

The conversation continued with the psychiatrist asking me all sorts of questions. I later found out my answers were all characteristics of not just disordered eating but an actual eating disorder for someone who restricts and compensates. I have to be honest, the conversation that day was a bit blurry. She called my husband into the room after they did the EKG. She explained to us both that her recommendation was inpatient, today. Literally that moment, she wanted me to sign myself into the eating disorder unit, hand over my cell phone, and say goodbye to my husband.

"That's not going to work for me. I have three kids. I can't go without seeing them or even speaking to them on the phone."

My husband jumped in and asked what he could do at home to help me so I didn't have to stay. The doctor replied to him quite frankly, saying there was nothing he could do and that I had "TO EAT" on my own. That would need to be medically supervised and, therefore, inpatient was the only option.

"Can I go home for Easter?"

"No."

"How long will I be here?"

"We never know. Usually a month or so."

A month! Was she insane? I am a mother of three kids, one being a baby. I have a house and a husband. I can't just abort my life and head to the ED unit for a month.

"Thank you for your time, but this isn't for me. Have a nice day."

The doctor put it all on the table as I walked out the door to leave. To sum it up, she told me this: I was sick. I was very sick. My BMI was concerning, my bloodwork was falling within dangerous levels and my conversation with her was concerning. I had a hard time answering her questions, and it seemed to her it was hard for me to concentrate. This led her to believe I had a lack of oxygen to my brain due to the low white blood cells. I could never fight an infection with this level of WBC, and EVEN IF I promised to start eating again, I would be in great danger to do this without supervision. My organs had slowed down so much that pushing them too hard too quickly could actually cause that organ to fail. I would most likely experience refeeding syndrome, and that needed to be monitored. I would go back and forth from freezing to sweating. My stomach would bloat, causing me to want to stop eating. I would also have digestive issues, and the hardest part, tackling the mental aspect of this, couldn't be done without them.

"I know you don't want to stay, but I can offer this option if it gets you here every day. I can admit you under partial hospitalization. You will drive here every morning. You will eat your meals here, and you will stay the entire day. You can go home at night to see your kids but ONE incident, and you have to stay in the unit." She walked out of the room, and I spoke with my husband. He agreed this was the best choice for me.

The next day I arrived at the hospital for partial hospitalization in the eating disorder unit. I was greeted by the kindest lady, who saved my life in so many ways. It was her job to weigh me and take my vitals every day. She didn't mess around, but she did it in such a kind and motherly way. First order of business, shoes off, sweaters or hoodies off and you probably guessed it: scale time. I obviously couldn't see the numbers on the scale as she jotted them down in her secret notebook. It didn't bother me. I had already weighed myself twice before I got there. Next was blood pressure and heart rate. My BP was always super low. 70/55 was my average. It was like my heart couldn't wake up. When I was done, I headed into the unit. I was the oldest one there. Most of these boys and girls were in college. In the unit next to me were the adolescents. They were under 18. I was so embarrassed. Here I am in a room of a bunch of college kids, and I'm almost 40!

I sat down and had group therapy first thing every morning. After hearing the stories of the others, I swear I was in the wrong place. My heart never stopped, I never cut myself, I was never suicidal or septic or paralyzed. I just kept thinking, how am I here! I don't belong here. This was the result of a long line of confusion and people being overly dramatic. That day I had to complete two snacks and a lunch with them. The staff would take notes on our eating. How we ate, did we talk, were we silent, were we ritualistic, did we show signs of distress, did we complete the meals? The answer to that last question was a big fat NO. I was consuming 400-500 calories a day prior to being here, and now they place a piece of chicken and cauliflower and a chocolate brownie in front of me for lunch and expect me to eat it ALL. Not a chance. It was physically impossible. I was sweating. I had to keep stopping and taking deep breaths. I finally gave up. That first day I had incomplete meals on all my meals. I had gone through psychotherapy, one on one therapy, meetings with the dietician and psychiatrist, music therapy, art therapy and movement therapy, and I wanted to collapse with exhaustion. This was not for me. I cried the whole drive home.

But then something happened. By day three or four in group therapy, the group started talking about the way they thought about food. They started talking about their behaviors around food, and I realized these were the same thoughts I've been justifying in my head for years. We all literally THOUGHT THE SAME. It didn't matter how we got there. It didn't matter what our own traumas were, the eating disorder presents itself in similar ways. I could not believe these girls and boys had the same thought process as me around food. I was shocked to find out these weren't my own thoughts. Knowing that I had something in common with these people made it a lot easier to open up. The thing is, the more you open up emotionally, the more you literally open up old wounds and old traumas. Now I was not only trying to eat normal again, but I was emotionally processing years and years of life that affected me in ways I never knew.

My favorite therapist was the music therapist. She would play the guitar for us, and her voice warmed my heart while also chipping away at the wall I created around it. She always sang songs that were relatable in ways you didn't even realize. She made me go deep, and it was hard, but it worked. All my therapists were amazing. They taught me how to live again. They helped me move my body slightly so I wouldn't pass out, but I still got some good movement in (mostly stretches). The stories of success from the other members of my group were encouraging. On the days that people stopped showing up, I always wondered what happened to them, but mostly, I wondered if one day I would wake up and decide I didn't want to do this anymore. It was a roller coaster of emotions. Every. Single. Day. This wasn't the kind of therapy you went to for years and worked on trauma recovery and inner child work. This was the kind of fast-tracked therapy to get you to a healthy enough spot to be discharged AND THEN spend years with a therapist, psychiatrist and dietician to work your stuff out. The kind of therapy you got in the ED unit was meant to get to the root of the problem quickly. What I never knew or realized was how many things had been contributing factors to my mental illness, or ultimately, the eating disorder.

My trauma began with my car accident, followed by years of taunting and teasing, followed by a lack of feeling loved or seen, followed by abusive relationships, followed by deep betrayals, divorce and loss. Physically my body had gone through traumas that I never really allowed myself to process either. The car accident, hip surgery, brain surgery, and miscarriages were just a few. All of these things compiled together left me with a feeling of no self-worth and no self-esteem or value I held within myself. I made myself uncomfortable to make others comfortable. I lacked boundaries for fear of what others would feel if I put them in place. All of my traumas were also out of my control.

When Covid hit in 2020, I had just had my son. He had been born a few months prior and came down with a respiratory virus at five weeks old. We were admitted into the hospital with him and were there for his first Christmas. I didn't see my two older children for the first time ever on Christmas morning. As I was recovering emotionally from that, Covid hit. I spent the next two years of my life in isolation from everyone. No friends, no family. My husband developed severe anxiety and PTSD after the baby's hospitalization, and Covid only made it worse. He wanted to keep us all safe. The only way he knew how to do that was to keep us in a "bubble." In order to help with his illness, and I suppose a little of my own, we cut everyone off. This isolation is what pushed me over the edge. The lack of control put me in a downward spiral, stirring up old emotions and traumas I had refused to acknowledge in my previous years. I did my best for my family, but when my body physically gave out from restricting myself, I had to open up. I had to allow the help. I had to speak my truths. My sister in law took a picture of me in the hospital to remind me how far I have come. She only showed me that picture a year after my recovery, so I would never forget what I actually looked like at my lowest. I had never seen myself like that when I was sick. I did not see the balding on my scalp or the bones that stuck out so clearly. I didn't see my blue fingernails and dehydrated skin. What I saw was someone who could still lose a few pounds. I saw a person who fit into size zero pants, and I wanted it to stay that way.

A part of me still holds so much value in being small. The number on the scale, the size of my clothes, the size of my waist and hips, the size of my bra and my BMI number. I literally go to the doctors office and pay attention to the size cuff they are using on my arm. Adult small, it has to be adult small. In high school, I remember that my hip bones always had to be seen right above my pant line. There needed to be a small gap where the pants laid on my hip and across my stomach. At almost 40, not only was it important for my hip bone to show, but also my collar bone had to pop. We are talking about 25 years of obsessing over bones. That doesn't just go away in a few months. I won't pretend I am healed completely. I spent four months in the ED unit. On the days I wanted to quit, I thought about my kids with no mother and my husband with no wife. That kept me going, even if I wanted to kick and scream along the way. Ultimately, I was in recovery for them, which isn't the greatest reason.

What I Know Now

An eating disorder is nothing about the food and everything about mental health. The eating disorder resulted from me not taking care of my mental health. The eating disorder presented itself because I was having an internal struggle with something happening externally. Avoiding what was bothering me to keep a certain peace in my home or with particular family members was only poisoning me. Going to treatment for everyone else wasn't going to save me. I needed to WANT to be healthy. I needed to want to help myself. Self-care and self-love are two concepts that are so incredibly hard for people who grew up thinking they were worthless. How do you tell someone they deserve everything when they were told the opposite for the entirety of their life?

I wasn't completely sold on putting myself first, especially before my kids, but I had to go through the motions to get there mentally. I had to practice self-love and self-care every day until I finally got it. Without loving yourself, how can you expect others to love you? Without respecting yourself, how can you demand a certain level of respect from others? Without knowing your worth, how will you know if others are devaluing you or making you feel less than you are? To have healthy relationships with anyone in life and to maintain a good level of mental health, you must put yourself first in all capacities. It was only once I started working on healing the little girl inside me that felt unseen, unheard and unworthy, that I could start loving the pieces of me I thought were unlovable or broken. I silenced the mouths of those who made fun of me, bullied me and told that little girl how beautiful she was for so many other reasons. Once I told that little girl inside me that no matter what, I GOT YOU, and you don't need anyone else to help to feel seen or heard, I started to feel lighter. Once I told my younger self that she deserved better than the boy who cheated on her, or hit her, or emotionally abused her, I felt stronger. Once I told that little girl that she would do great things despite what her family thought of her, I felt empowered.

Working on the issues that have haunted you your whole life is no easy task. It's the hardest thing I have done in my life so far. It is, however, the only way that I started to heal. It's the only way I turned a life of being victimized and broken over and over into a life where I could put those pieces back together… confidently, nonetheless. The eating disorder unit my family chose for me saved my life. Not only was I discharged with all of my blood work within normal limits but I had reached my set weight and was thriving. My team at the hospital taught me how to be healthy again, but not just physically. They got to the root of the problem. An eating disorder is a symptom, not an illness. The team I had was able to help me explore what it was that was causing my need to control my food. They were able to give me the confidence I needed, the tools I needed, the support I needed and I am alive because of them. I am living my best life because of them. I did the work and on the days I wanted to quit they made sure to remind me that my life was worth saving. I miss my team and the people in treatment with me some days, but because of all of them, I will probably never have to see them again, a bittersweet thought. I bet you this. Once you've done the work—once you've learned how to care for yourself and love yourself and see your worth without limitations—you'll see that all those broken pieces of you actually make something beautiful.

The Lotus

So where am I now? A few months before my 40th birthday, I was discharged from the eating disorder unit. I had over 200 hours of therapy under my belt, and for the first time in my life, I slowly started to appreciate myself. I was slowly loving myself. I slowly understood what was acceptable in my life and what no longer served its purpose. I figured out who was worth having in my life, who never was and who never will be. But it was WORK. It took vulnerability, accountability, acceptance and perspective. I had to shift from thinking I was worthless to demanding respect and only allowing people to treat me at the level I would tolerate. It took talking about the things I thought I had forgotten about and talking about them out loud… to strangers. It took listening. It took reflecting. But believe me when I tell you, your mental health IS your health. If your mind and nervous system are not at peace, your entire health is at risk. You are worth all that hard work it will take to feel love for yourself. Even after being treated by an entire treatment team for four months, I will probably need therapy for life to continue to stay mentally healthy. There is absolutely nothing wrong with that. In fact, I would encourage everyone, struggling with their mental health or not, to see a therapist. It helps to hear yourself speak out loud or to see your words on paper.

After resigning from my teaching job during Covid, I found myself very unfulfilled. I knew I eventually wanted to have a career again, but

I had absolutely no idea what I wanted to do. I was 40 years old, and I still did not know what my passion was. I considered changing careers, I considered going back to college to take courses and continue my education in psychology, I considered going back to my old job or starting a new job in a new school district. For a short time, I helped with interior design in my husband's business, which was fun, but I was still missing something that made me feel fulfilled. I was fortunate enough to be able to work for a family member from home. This helped me a lot mentally because when the big kids were in school and my little guy started daycare, it gave some purpose to my days. I felt alive in a sense that I was motivated and completing tasks while communicating with other adults. However, this was not the entire picture of what I wanted out of life. As I continued to work on my writing, just as a journaling activity for after treatment, the lightbulb went off. I knew my story was my purpose. I knew I had to finish this book and get it in the hands of others. I knew I lived through all of these things and came out better so I could help others do the same. As I dedicated myself to completing this book, I finally felt proud, accomplished, fulfilled and excited in a way no other career or job has ever made me feel. When I signed the contract to publish this book, my emotions were triggered in such a good way! Never in a million years would I have thought this would be my job…but when you do the work of self-exploration, you'll find things that you never knew existed inside of you. You'll find yourself pleasantly surprised.

I challenge you to go deep into those memories that have caused the wounds on your soul and heart and explore the WHYs of how you feel. This will be so hard. It will take time and conflict in your mind. Take it easy on yourself. Only explore these wounds at a pace you can handle with the support you need to do it. Doing this instead of covering it up with some mind-numbing activity will release the poison you've been keeping inside all this time.

When your brain is focused on the negative, that is what you get in return. Thinking negatively will eventually turn your hurt into anger and rage. Instead, change your perspective. Reject what they have done to you. Prove them wrong! There is no place for this in your life. There is no place for this if you are searching for peace and to grow as a person. Forgive them. Finding your own peace will depend on your ability to do this. Holding a grudge or ill feelings towards someone who has done you wrong is poisoning yourself.

You may have heard the saying that through all darkness grows new things. The lotus is a very delicate, beautiful flower that grows out of extreme darkness. I like to think we can all be a form of the lotus. Through our darkest times, we must remember it's because we are about to grow into something new and beautiful. It could even be said that a person dies a hundred times in one lifetime. That the person they were is no longer. The person they once were dies in that darkness, but something new grows. Something better and beautiful. You shed the skin of your old life and create a new one. All those years of heartache were not wasted. You may have been broken so often in life that you very well could have just called it quits. But you're here, reading this, so I know there is a seed sprouting somewhere inside you, waiting for your next chapter. But please know this, each tear was not lost. Each tear is a drop collected in a bucket. That bucket gives you growth, a different mindset, higher standards, more self-worth and more appreciation for the things you have to offer. The tears and grief make you wiser and stronger. Without the tears, your soul would be empty. The tears are what make up a part of you. The tears are the water that heals you and allows your soul growth and your heart to become stronger. And one day, it will all make sense. One day all those cracks and chips, all the things that shattered you to the core, all the curveballs that you thought broke you, will ironically be all the things that make you whole... all the things that make you beautifully broken.

Liar Liar Pants On Fire

Throughout my whole life, I heard dozens of sayings that people spew out of their mouths like word vomit. Most of the time, it's when they don't have any real advice to give or they are at a loss for words. These sayings are like what people keep in their back pocket and pull out at whatever time they feel applies. The problem is these phrases are thrown around without any real thought to their implications. If a person really thought about the words and how they applied to the particular person they were speaking to, there is a high chance they would choose a different saying. So, here we go. Something to think about the next time someone says them to you, or maybe even something for you to think about before using them.

1. You're so strong OR *After everything you've been through, you can certainly get through this* OR *I could never survive what you did.*

THIS IS ONE OF MY LEAST FAVORITE. Yes, I know I have been through many of life's curveballs, tornadoes, shit storms, tragedies, whatever you want to call them. People don't ever ask the universe to test them in such a way to prove their strength. No one wants to go through hell just to be called strong. We didn't ask to be strong. We were forced to be. And never in a million years would I say that being called "strong" was worth everything I went through. I am strong, not by some magical wand the universe waved at me, but

from broken to beautifully broken

because I HAD TO BE. Life threw me in the pit, and I had no choice but to survive. I got dealt a bad hand, fell into a series of unfortunate events—however you want to say it. I was forced to deal with something, and in the end, I survived. Did it necessarily make me stronger? I don't think so. I think some things made me weaker, more vulnerable, isolated, fearful, worrisome and anxious. But stronger isn't really the word that comes to mind. I don't know who made this saying up, but please make it stop.

2. It could always be worse OR *Be thankful it wasn't any worse* OR *I had it so much worse than you and blah blah blah.*

Yes, I am very aware it could have been worse. It could always be worse in any situation, HOWEVER, that doesn't make my experience any less traumatic or painful or real. This phrase downplays and minimizes my journey, and I don't appreciate that. I have the right to express myself, and the level of anything I feel should not be compared to someone else's experience.

3. *You are so lucky for the life you have* OR *You are so #blessed.*

This one makes my whole body burn with hives. THIS IS NOT LUCK. This life I created didn't happen by some divine intervention. I worked for this shit. I worked hard. I made this life what it is. I started from beneath rock bottom and climbed my way up. I fell quite a few times and started over. I calculated my life after my mistakes and all the bad hands I was dealt. I figured out how I would live the life I wanted and was determined to get there. No one BLESSED me with this. It wasn't LUCK. You all need to stop with that nonsense like the universe will just hand you a silver platter of a perfect life without an ounce of effort. Not blessed. Not lucky. Determined. Driven. Focused. Accountable. Perceptive. Patient. Understanding. Empathetic. Smart.

4. Life is just too short to hold a grudge, especially with family.

Okay yes, sometimes life is too short for nonsense. Life is too short to waste my time on things that don't better me or make me a better person. HOWEVER, if I mention I'm not speaking to a certain family member or old friend, please don't tell me life is too short to stay mad. No, you have it all wrong. Life IS too short to allow myself to be present in situations where I'm uncomfortable or becoming the victim of narcissistic abuse or any other kind of mental abuse. Life is too short to spend time with anyone who doesn't appreciate me in all my rawness, all my flaws and all my cracks. Life is too short to be around people who make me feel less.

5. She totally let herself go.

When someone says this referring to another woman, they are implying that said woman is not keeping up with society's standards of beauty. Maybe her weight has changed or she stopped dying her hair. Maybe she started wearing more comfortable clothes and stopped putting on makeup. The next time you are tempted to say this about another woman, think about this: maybe she LET HERSELF GO. Maybe she untied her hands from the unattainable standards society sets. Maybe she decided she wanted to unbind herself from having to be so much for so many people. And maybe SHE LET HERSELF GO FREE!

6. What doesn't kill you makes you stronger.

What doesn't kill me actually only did just that. That's all there is to it. I didn't ask to be put in a situation that would put me near the brink of death just to say, "Wow, that was a close one, thankfully I'm stronger now." No one wants to get thrown in the lion's den, and come out to say, "That was all worth it 'cause I'm stronger now." I'm worn out, tired, stressed, exhausted, both mentally and physically, but the last thing I feel is stronger.

7. Everything happens for a reason.

Not everything in life has a reason. Sometimes we have bad times out of our control, and that's it. Sometimes we can learn something from those bad times, but there was no reason we had to go through that bad time in the first place. When people say that, they imply that something I'm going through is supposed to happen to me. By saying, "Everything happens for a reason," they are saying I have no control over where my life goes. They're saying the universe causes things to happen to me for a reason. It's actually the opposite. I control what happens in my life. I ask the universe for what I want.

8. It will all work out OR It is what it is.

When you say either of these two phrases, it can unintentionally cause the person to throw their hands up and say whatever happens, happens. They become reactive instead of proactive. They think that the universe will just work out their problems or they are just supposed to accept the problem when in reality, the saying should be something like: *It will all work out if you keep working toward your goal* OR *It is what it is if you decide to give up and do nothing.* Something can only stay the way "it is" if no effort is put toward changing it.

9. If you don't have anything nice to say, don't say anything at all.

Sometimes though, things that aren't "nice," are necessary. Staying quiet might cause more harm than simply phrasing the comment in a way that isn't rude but gets the point across. There's a way to say anything as long as you use the correct tone and delivery.

Here's the biggest reason people should never say this awful saying. It teaches children that they should silence their voices if they think someone might not like what they have to say. Not everyone will like what you have to say, and that's okay. Don't ever silence your opinions or your thoughts. Use your voice.

10. *You look beautiful today,* OR *you look like you lost weight, you look great,* OR *You're so skinny, I'm so jealous!*

We literally never know what someone is battling. When we tell someone who is restricting their food intake that they look beautiful because they lost a few pounds, what we're doing without knowing is fueling that restriction. The more external validation they get when restricting, the more they think it's okay. On the other hand, someone may have lost weight because they are ill and aren't trying to lose weight. Here's another thought many people have not considered. When you tell someone they look beautiful today, if they have any kind of body dysmorphia or disordered eating or self-destructive behaviors, their brain can internalize that as, *all the OTHER days, I didn't look beautiful.* The next time you see them, they will expect you to say the same, and if you don't, they will assume something is wrong with them.

Here's the solution. No one means for these societally created compliments to offend a person. Their intention is the opposite, to make someone feel good about themselves. What if we try something altogether different? What if we compliment a person on anything else BUT the way they look? Compliment an accomplishment they recently had, compliment their opinions in a conversation, or even just compliment their smile. Compliment anything that doesn't have to do with their bodies! Let's change what society puts the most pressure on everyone to do—look good! Let's create a societal standard that's attainable, BE GOOD. Just be good people. Period.

11. *After all I've done for you.*

Has somebody ever said "After all I've done for you" in response to you declining to do something for them or treating them in some way they see unfit? If so, then, unfortunately, the person who is saying this to you did not do any act of kindness towards you to be a good person. They did that particular act of kindness or favor for you with the expectation that you now owe them something. What they're saying is, they kept a list of everything they've ever done for you, and now that you don't abide by what they want you to do, they are simply saying they should have never done those things for you. They were never done out of the kindness of their heart. They were never done because they were good people. They were done because they put these things in their back pocket for use later on in life to get you to do something for them. It was an unwritten contract that you now owe them. Stay very far away from people who use this saying.

12. Big kids don't cry.

This was a hard one for me because I found myself using it with my own children. By telling our children that big kids don't cry, we're insinuating that adults don't show emotion. What we're ultimately saying is that only babies cry, and once we get enough knowledge, we understand that crying is not the answer. So as a child, when they feel like crying is not something they are supposed to do, they will take that into adulthood and feel shame when they do have to cry. This statement could not be farther from the truth. The healthiest thing a person can do is cry when they feel like crying. Letting out your emotion is the only way it doesn't eat you up inside. If you were to bottle up all that sadness and never let it out, it would eventually turn to anger. And so by saying big kids don't cry, we're creating this narrative for children to become angry adults. Next time you're tempted to tell your child that big kids don't cry just to get your child to stop crying, try something new. Ask them why they are upset. Ask them why they are crying. Ask them to use their words. Ask them if there is a way that you can help them feel better. Have a conversation instead of just dismissing the emotion so that the crying stops and you can move on.

I hope that you have enjoyed reading what my journey through this thing called life has been so far. I hope that if you are suffering in some way, this will give you a push to find your voice and make the next move towards being your best self. If you are someone who knows a person who may be suffering in some way, I hope that my journey has provided a level of enlightenment that you will use to further educate yourself on the facts of mental health so that you can be the support system your loved one needs. You can be a positive part of their journey through recovery. I hope that I was, in some capacity, a part of all of your healing journeys.

About the Author

Ella Shae was born into your average family that loved and cared for her in every capacity possible. Her journey with mental health awareness, unbeknownst to her, began at an early age of 4 years old after a car accident that could have killed her but instead left her with lasting scars. As the years progressed in her journey, so did the traumas, and in turn, so did her challenges with her mental health. It wasn't until a compilation of many mental health struggles presented themselves as an eating disorder that Ella finally received the proper treatment to work through 35 years of trauma.

After months of therapy in all different shapes and forms, Ella was finally able to reopen her old wounds that had been haunting her. She learned that trauma does not have to make you a victim. All these things in life that she thought had made her a victim could actually help her to grow into the best version of herself. All those years that she thought life was digging her into this deeper and darker hole just needed to be looked at from a new perspective. She learned to pull the life lesson out of all the things that she had thought broke her. Life had actually given her the possibility to grow.

Today, Ella has a husband who supports her and nourishes her on the days that can sometimes be a little challenging. Recovery from anything is not linear, so having a family that supports her is her greatest gift. Her three children are her proudest accomplishments, and every day she continues to learn and grow with them.

Ella continues to be the voice for the unspoken and the face for the unseen. Her hope is that anyone who reads this finds their own voice to be heard and that they can find a relatable moment. She wants every reader to know they are not alone, whether they are suffering in silence or are someone who needs to be a part of a support system for someone else.

Ella has an educational background in teaching and psychology. As a teacher, Ella ran the Sources Of Strength Club, which guided peers to help other peers during challenging times. She was also the founder and creator of Family STEM Challenges (Science, Technology, Engineering, and Math) in her home town and surrounding towns provided a chance for family bonding. She is currently on the Fashion with Compassion Committee that raises funds for a children's hospital and is currently available for Trauma Life Coaching.

To learn more about Ella and how she can help you or someone you love who may be struggling, visit www.ellashae.com.

ella shae
AUTHOR

Need Immediate Assistance? Dial 988 from any phone to connect to the National Suicide Prevention and Mental Health Crisis Lifeline. This is a free service available through chat, text or phone for substance use crisis, emotional distress and more.

About Ella Shae: Visit www.ellashae.com to learn more about Ella Shae, a trauma-informed coach specializing in eating disorder recovery or email info@ellashae.com.

Connect with Ella: For bookings, media appearances, interviews, motivational speaking or a consultation with Ella for Trauma Informed Coaching, email info@ellashae.com.

Sending love and light to all.